CHESTER'S MILITARY HERITAGE

Adrian and Dawn L. Bridge

AMBERLEY

First published 2021

Amberley Publishing
The Hill, Stroud
Gloucestershire, GL5 4EP

www.amberley-books.com

Logo source material courtesy of Gerry van Tonder

ISBN 978 1 4456 9958 5 (print)
ISBN 978 1 4456 9959 2 (ebook)

British Library Cataloguing in Publication Data.
A catalogue record for this book is available from the British Library.

Origination by Amberley Publishing.
Printed in Great Britain.

Contents

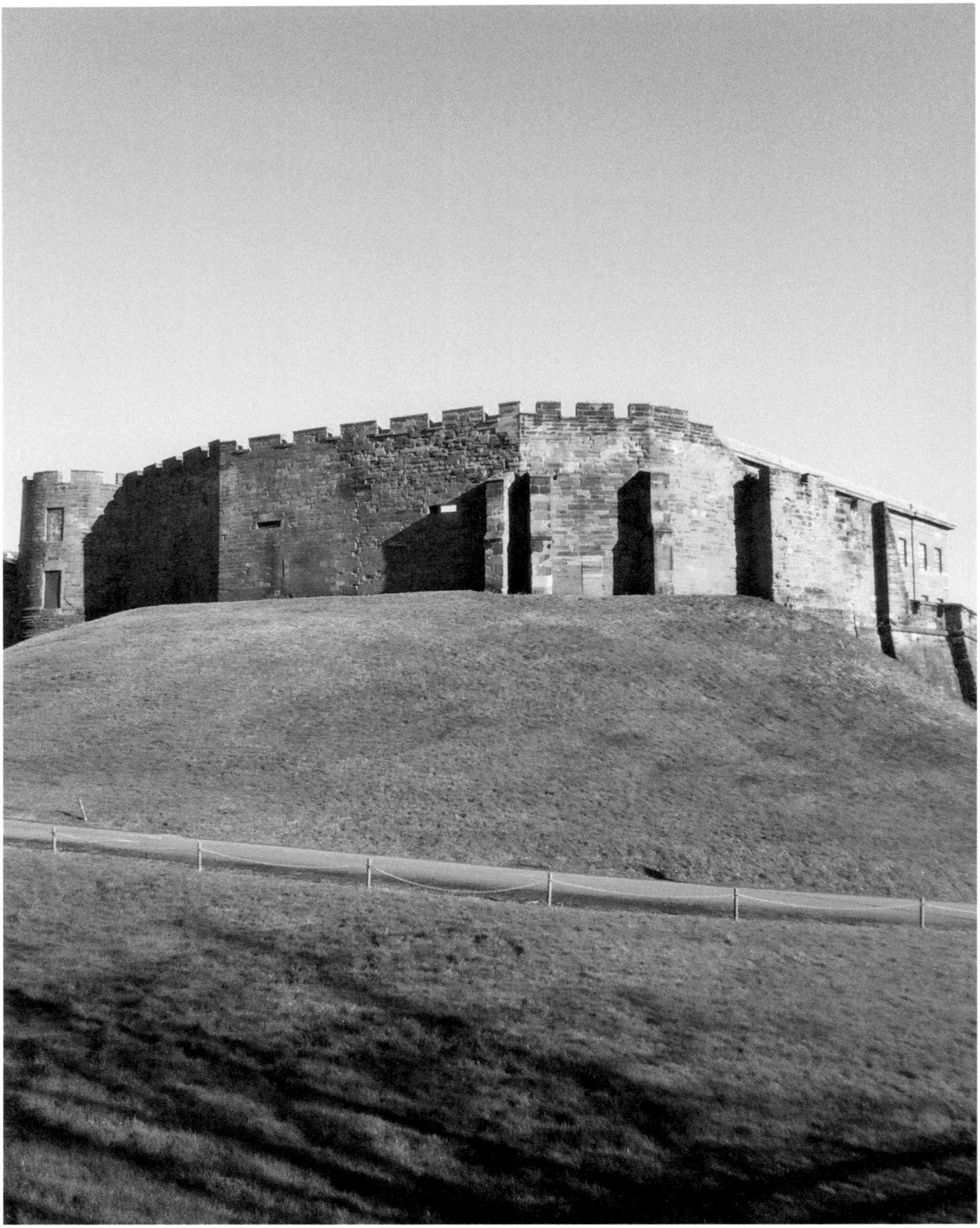

Introduction

Chester's long and illustrious military heritage stretches back nearly 2,000 years to the CE 70s, when the Roman legions first began to build a fortress on the banks of the River Dee. This fortress, and the civilian settlement that soon grew up beside it, was named Deva (almost certainly after the river) though in the subsequent centuries of Roman domination the town was often known as Deva Victrix, in honour of the Victrix Roman legion, which was based in the area from the first to the fourth centuries CE.

The settlement established at Deva remained important even after the Romans had left the country. Under the Anglo-Saxons, Deva became known as Legacaestir – 'fortress-city of the legions' – which was shortened to 'Caestir', and then over time into the modern 'Chester'. The Anglo-Saxons fortified and garrisoned Legacaestir/Caestir, as did the Normans in the period after 1066. During the Middle Ages Chester retained its military significance as a gathering point and victualling base for English forces intent on the subjugation of Wales. In the era of the Tudor and Stuart monarchs, Chester was also a key launching pad for English military forays into Ireland. The city's military importance declined somewhat during the eighteenth century but rose again in the nineteenth and twentieth centuries as a result of army regionalisation policies and the impact of two world wars. Chester's continued military importance in this period owed much to its strategic geographical position. The city on the banks of the Dee was at a key crossroads of the British Isles, dominating land routes into northern Wales, and sea routes to Ireland and the coastal parts of western Scotland. Right into Hanoverian times, Chester was an important staging post to Ireland, being roughly equidistant between London (185 miles away) and Dublin (150 miles across the Irish Sea).

For much of its history, Chester was also a major west coast port. The original Roman port facilities were expanded considerably during the subsequent centuries, and despite the fact that the Dee Estuary began to silt up in the Middle Ages, Chester's access to the Irish Sea remained a key reason for the city's strategic importance for well over 1,500 years.

For many centuries, Chester was undoubtedly the most important town in north-west England. It dominated an economic hinterland that included west Cheshire and north-east Wales, and it was the county town of Cheshire. Indeed, such was Chester's dominance in north-western England between the fourteenth and eighteenth centuries that the town was often known as Westchester. Nevertheless, despite these factors, for most of its history Chester remained a remarkably small place. Between the fourteenth century and the beginning of the nineteenth century, the whole town was probably encompassed within little more than 3,000 acres, stretching from the abbot of Chester's manor in the north towards Handbridge in the south, and by 1700 its total population was probably less than 8,000 people. Chester only really began to expand in the 1840s,

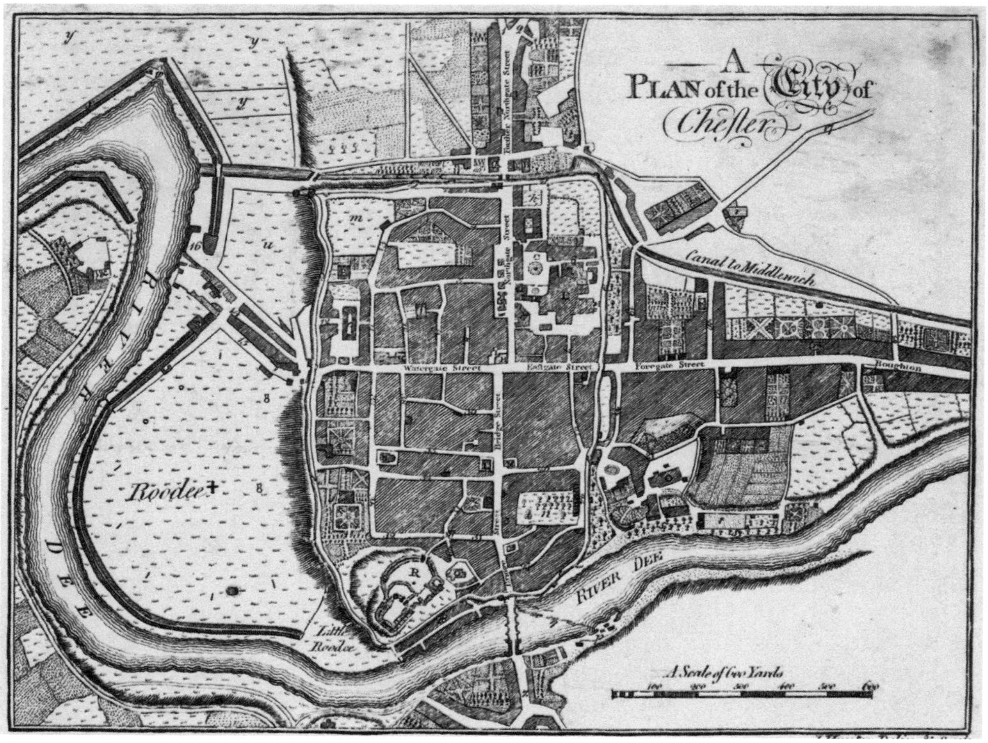

Thomas Pennant's 1781 map of Chester. (© National Library of Wales)

with the arrival of the railways, and in the twentieth century the city boundaries were also expanded to include areas such as Great Boughton, Newton, Blacon, Hoole, Upton and Bache.

For such a comparatively small city, Chester has left a massive military imprint. During the course of the past 2,000 years, military personnel from all over the world have walked its streets, and those born in Chester have left the city to fight in many of the world's great conflicts. Chester itself has also been at the centre of a number of major armed clashes. During the course of the following pages, the military organisations, individuals, battles, sieges and plots that together make up the rich martial heritage of Chester will be explored in some detail. It is, in many respects, an epic tale involving countless examples of courage, service and sacrifice, which we hope you find both enjoyable and informative.

1. Deva's Roman Legions

One of the great fighting legions of Ancient Rome, Legio Secunda Adiutrix (which roughly translates as the 'Rescuer Second Legion'), was almost certainly responsible for the building of the first fort at Deva, during the CE 70s, when the legion was participating in the Roman governor Agricola's campaigns to extend imperial control into the north of Britannia, Wales and Caledonia. Legio II Adiutrix was created by the emperor Vespasian – in CE 70 – and was originally composed of marines from the imperial Roman navy. It therefore seems logical that these former marines would be given the job of creating the military base, and its key port facilities, at Deva on the banks of the River Dee.

Following its formation in CE 70, II Adiutrix established its sound fighting credentials by crushing the Batavian revolt in the province of Germania Inferior, on the western banks of the River Rhine. Germany was a tough posting for Roman legionaries, and by the time II Adiutrix came to Britain in CE 71 the legion was full of seasoned, battle-hardened warriors. During the legion's subsequent sixteen years in the province of Britannia,

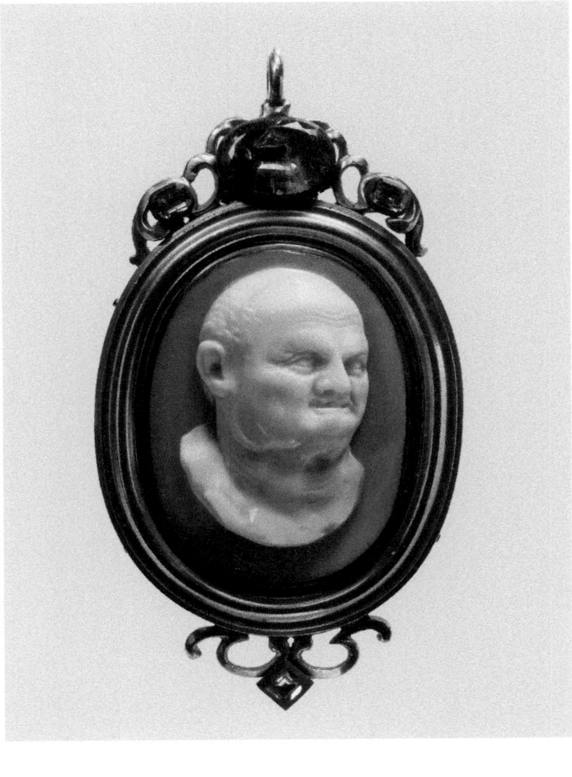

Emperor Vespasian gold cameo.
(© Metropolitan Museum of Art)

building a fort and settlement at Deva was just one of its many responsibilities. However, the legion's stay in the Roman Empire's most northerly province was cut short in CE 87, when II Adiutrix was transferred to eastern Europe to fight in Rome's Dacian wars, along the River Danube. The legion never returned to Deva, or Britannia, though it remained a distinguished fighting cog in the overall Roman war machine, and the future emperor, Hadrian, became one of its very best commanders (as military tribune).

The Roman legion most synonymous with ancient Deva was undoubtedly Legio XX Valeria Victrix. One literal translation of the Latin word 'Valeria' would be 'black eagle' with 'Victrix' meaning 'victorious'. However, judging from the scale and nature of relevant tomb and other inscriptions, the XXth Legion remained without a title for some time, and was known as just the XXth Victrix Legion on many occasions. These particular legionaries took over from the men of II Adiutrix in CE 88 and began replacing the initial wooden palisades and fortifications of Deva with brick and stone from the nearby settlement at Holt. The XXth Legion was to stay with a base at Deva for at least the next 200 years. Prior to its arrival on the banks of the River Dee in CE 88, the XXth Victrix had already blazed a campaigning trail across other parts of Britannia and across areas of Continental Europe.

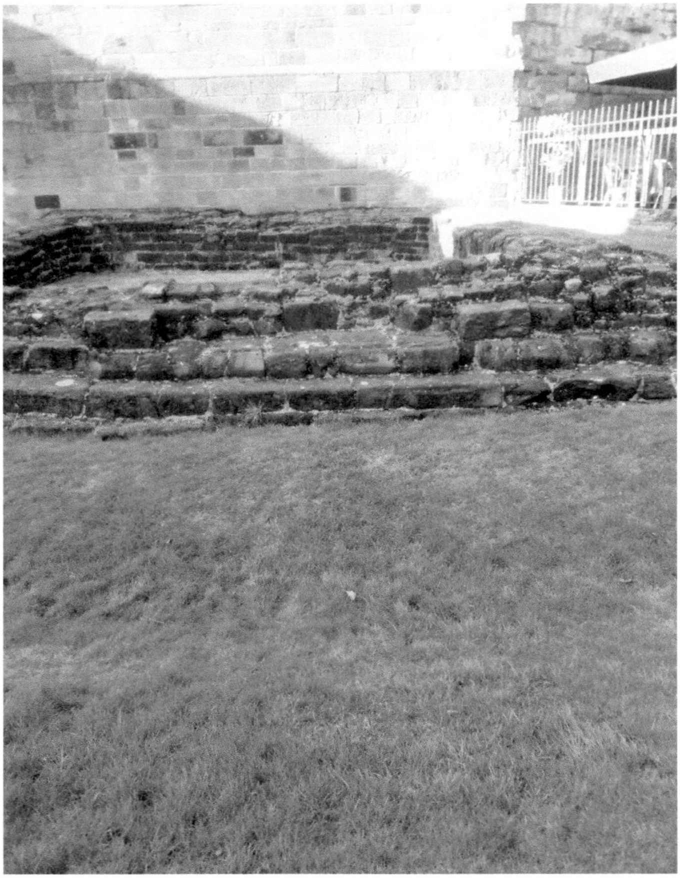

Foundations of Roman tower built at Deva *c.* CE 74–96.

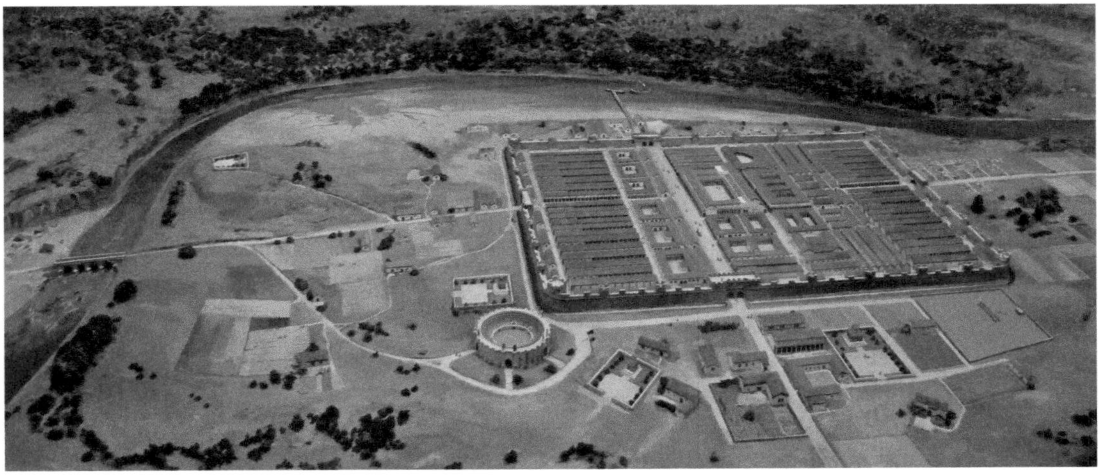

Model reconstruction of Deva. (Courtesy of Lukasz Nurczynski)

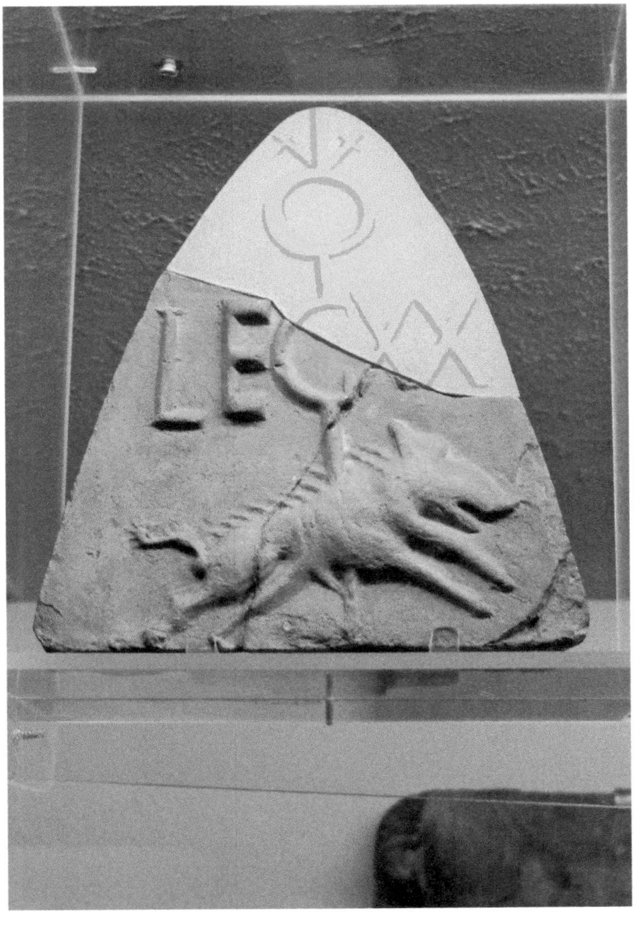

Roman tile with XXth Legion wild boar emblem. (Courtesy of Wolfgang Sauber)

The first Roman emperor, Augustus (formerly Octavian), had founded the new legion shortly after 31 BCE, and it soon saw action in Hispania, Germany, and along the River Danube. In CE 43, Valeria Victrix was one of the four legions chosen by Emperor Claudius to spearhead the invasion of Britain. Subsequently, the legion was involved in fighting on a wide range of fronts, even before it based itself at Deva. It helped crush King Caractacus' forces at the Battle of Caer Caradoc, and assisted in the conquest of the Silures tribe of Wales during the CE 50s. In CE 60–61 Valeria Victrix helped annihilate Queen Boudica's Iceni and other warriors in the climactic battle of the Boudican revolt, along Watling Street, and it also marched into Anglesey to destroy the power of the Druids. Between CE 78 and 84 the XXth Victrix legion carried its standards into battle against various foes (during Agricola's campaigns in northern Britannia and Caledonia) before finally settling into its new fortified base at Deva. While most Victrix legionaries moved to Deva after fighting with Agricola, a detachment from the same legion was also involved in crushing a rebellion on the Continent – in Gaul – before heading to their new home on the banks of the River Dee. For the next 200 years the XXth Legion was often on the move, leaving only a skeleton garrison behind it in Deva.

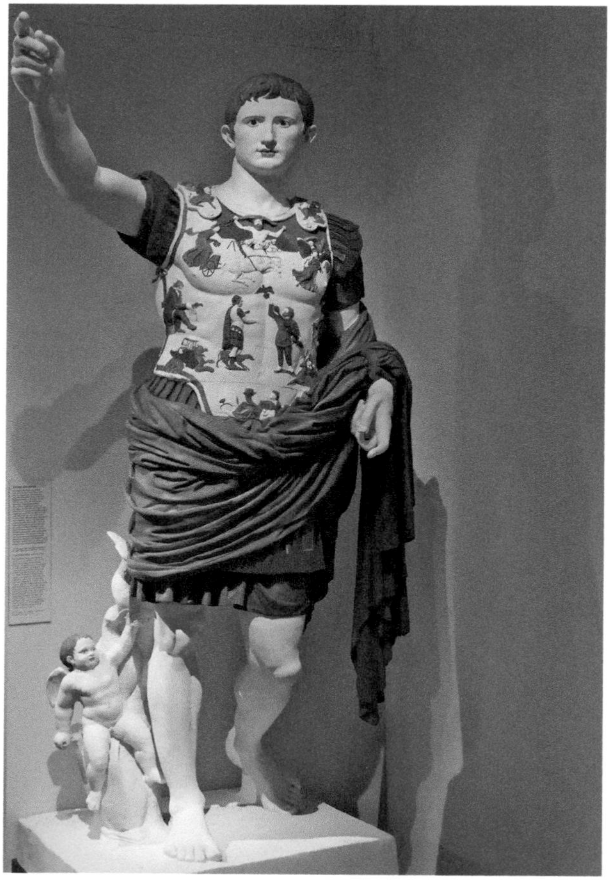

Emperor Augustus, founder of the XXth Legion. (© Allard Pierson Museum)

XXth Victrix was one of the legions involved in constructing Hadrian's Wall, and it also had some involvement in the creation of the more northerly Antonine's Wall. Much of the Deva-based legion was also probably on the march in Gaul in CE 196, supporting the failed bid of Clodius Albinus to become emperor of Rome. Towards the end of the third century CE, the XXth was still a significant military presence in Britain, but after this period evidence for the presence of this famous fighting legion is difficult to find. The legion may well still have been present until Roman forces were pulled out of Britain in CE 407. Conversely, it could have been disbanded on an earlier occasion. In any event, Legio XX Valeria Victrix left behind enough traces of its existence to provide a rich contribution to the military heritage of Chester.

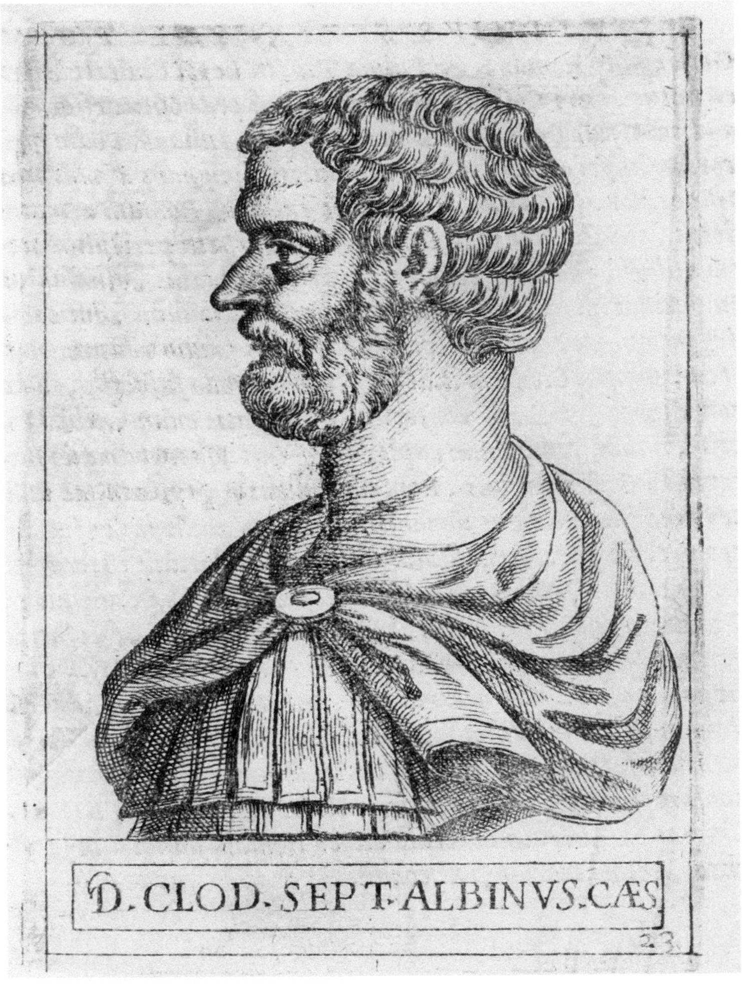

A 1583 illustration of Clodius Albinus. (© Municipal Library of Trento)

2. From Henry Howard to the Mercians

Once the Romans had departed from the shores of Britain, it was to be a very long time indeed before Deva (and the later town of Chester) had a sustained link with any particular military units. Saxons and Vikings came and went from the city, Norman forces were based within the castle keep, and Cheshire archers and soldiers passed through Chester on their way to fight in various Welsh and Irish wars. However, it wasn't until the end of the seventeenth century that the city again struck up strong links with a military unit that were in any way comparable to the links between ancient Deva and the Valeria Victrix Roman Legion. In 1689, Henry Howard, the 7th Duke of Norfolk, raised a regiment of foot soldiers at the Roodee in Chester in support of the new joint monarchs, William and Mary. Over time, the regiment became known as the 22nd Foot, and later as the Cheshire Regiment, and it provided over 300 years of unbroken service to the Crown, before being merged into the newly formed Mercian Regiment in 2007.

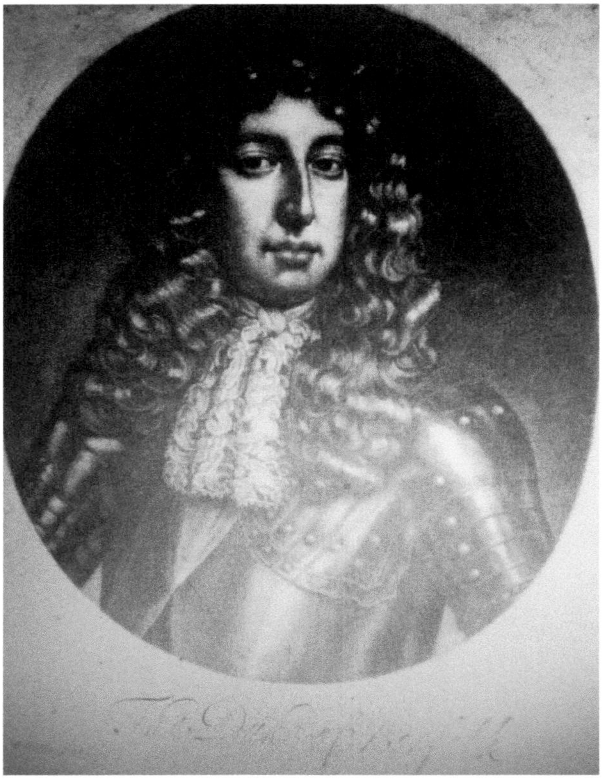

Henry Howard, 7th Duke of Norfolk, by Peter Lely.

Howard's new regiment was founded at a time of acute political turmoil. James II was a Catholic king of England and had been toppled from power in the so-called Glorious Revolution of 1688 by his Protestant daughter Mary and his son-in-law, William of Orange. By 1689, James II had landed in Ireland (with French military support) in order to begin the process of reclaiming the throne of England from William and Mary. Henry Howard's new Chester-raised regiment was formed in order to defend the new regime of William and Mary, and to help fight off the nearby threat of James II in Ireland. The new regiment, raised at the Roodee, was very much seen as being Henry Howard's own personal property. Until well into the eighteenth century, regiments bore the names of those that commanded them.

Although Henry Howard bears the distinction of founding the formation that later became known as the Cheshire Regiment, he didn't stay in charge for long. In September 1689, Sir Henry Belasyse took over as the colonel in charge of the new regiment, which henceforward became known as Belasyse's Regiment of Foot. Belasyse's regiment fought in Ireland, and in Europe, until a peace treaty was agreed with Louis XIV in 1697. Once a European peace had been declared, the English government was no longer keen to fund a large standing army. As a result, the Belasyse Regiment of Foot could well have been disbanded, had it not found favour with the separate Irish government, which funded Belasyse's men from its own resources. The regiment was posted to Jamaica in 1701, where it spent the following twelve years. Such a posting (when looked at from a twenty-first-century perspective) might have seemed rather idyllic; however, in the eighteenth century a military tour in the disease-ridden West Indies was decidedly unwelcome. At various points in the eighteenth century, roughly 10 per cent of all British soldiers posted to the Caribbean died en route before they'd even set foot on land. A posting to Jamaica, therefore, was not an enticing prospect for many, and it was no surprise that Belasyse failed to accompany his men to the West Indies and instead transferred the colonelcy of his regiment to William Selwyn.

Belasyse's concerns about being based in Jamaica may well seem more justified in view of the fact that his successor, Selwyn, died almost immediately – in April 1702. For the next twenty-eight years, the regiment was run by the Handasyd family. Thomas Handasyd took over as Selwyn's successor and also became governor of Jamaica, and between 1712 and 1730 Thomas's son, Roger, acted as colonel of the regiment. However, by 1751, the era of the regiment being named after its colonel was at an end, and the military unit originally formed in Chester became known as the 22nd Regiment of Foot.

Fighting the French was a recurring theme for the regiment throughout much of the eighteenth century. In 1743, one detachment fought at the Battle of Dettingen, in Bavaria, against both French and Bavarian forces, during the War of the Austrian Succession. The Battle of Dettingen was the last occasion on which a British monarch (George II) was present in person to lead his troops in action. During the fighting, it appears that the king may well have been sheltered under an oak tree by men from the regiment. As a reward for their assistance in the battle, George presented the detachment with a sprig of oak leaves. This oak leaf symbol became a precious part of the regimental standard for the 22nd Foot, and then the Cheshire Regiment, for the next 300 years.

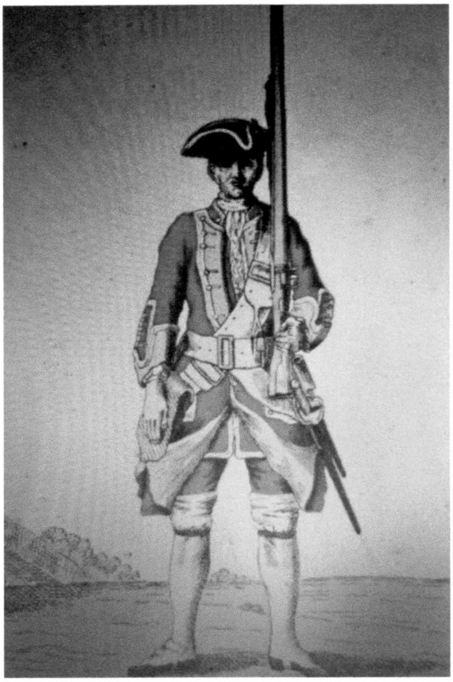

Left: Soldier from the 22nd Foot *c.* 1742, unknown artist.

Below: George II at Dettingen, by John Wootton, 1743. (© National Army Museum)

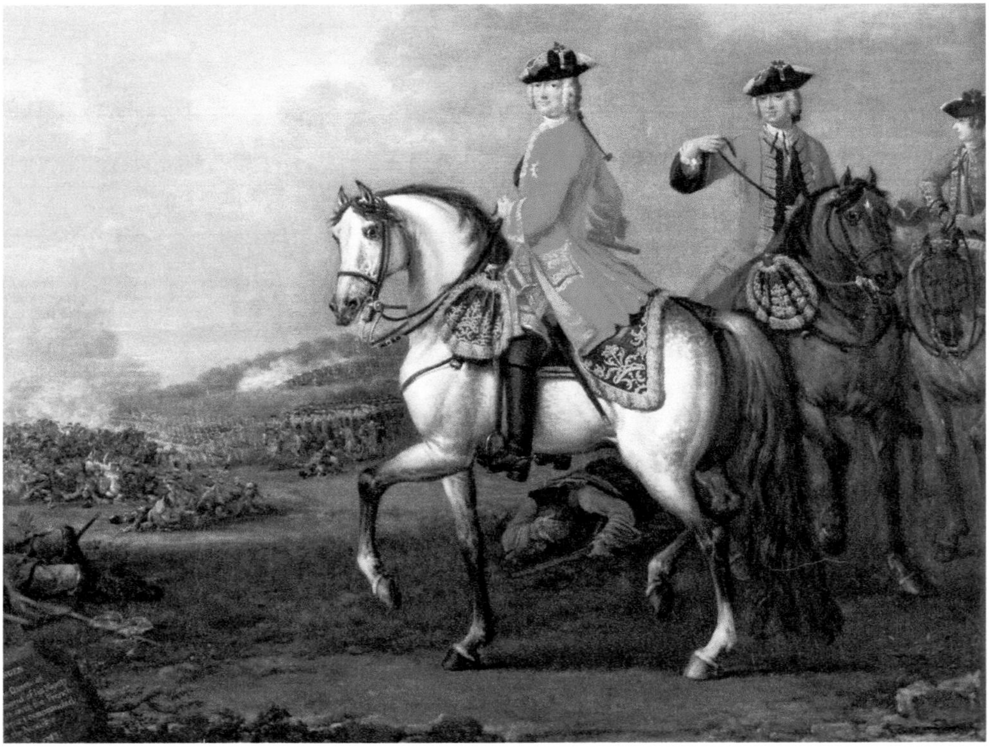

The 22nd Foot played a significant role in the creation and maintenance of what might be called the first British Empire, which was very much focused on the Caribbean and north America. During the Seven Years' War of the 1750s, the regiment helped dislodge the French from Canada, participating in the siege of Louisberg and also scaling the Heights of Abraham as part of General Wolfe's army, which subsequently defeated French forces in a parade-ground-style battle outside Quebec in 1759. In the early 1760s, the regiment was also used to assault Martinique and Cuba, and in 1775 the 22nd was shipped to the east coast of America in order to begin the fight against rebellious colonists seeking their independence from Britain. The regiment went on to play a noteworthy role in the American War of Independence, experiencing both victory and defeat in its struggles against the rebel colonists. The 22nd Foot disembarked just in time to participate in the 1775 British defeat at Bunker Hill, in which the regiment's commander, Lieutenant-Colonel James Abercrombie, was killed. After this, the 22nd was evacuated to Canada, before returning to fight in the New York area in 1778. Here, at the Battle of Newport, on Rhode Island, the regiment played its part in securing a rare strategic British military victory against the Americans. Despite the strategic triumph at Newport, the overall British position remained precarious, and the American colonies were lost forever when the British armies under Lord Cornwallis finally surrendered to the Americans at Yorktown, in 1781.

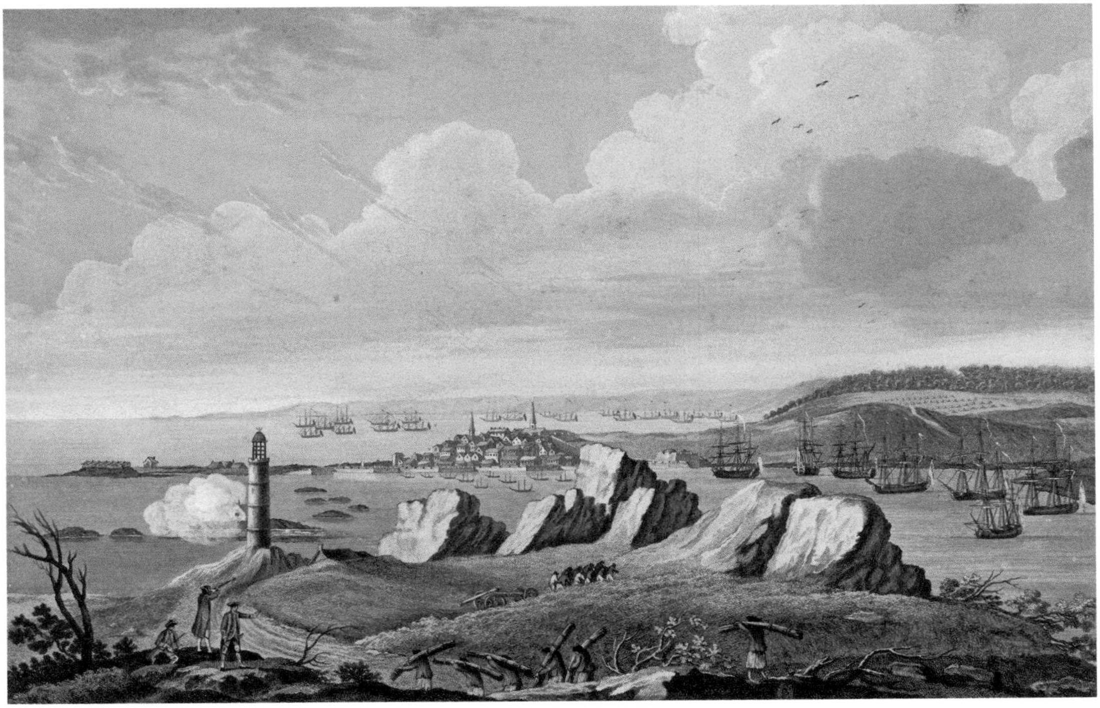

Siege of Louisberg, Canada, in 1758, by Pierre-Charles Canot, 1762.

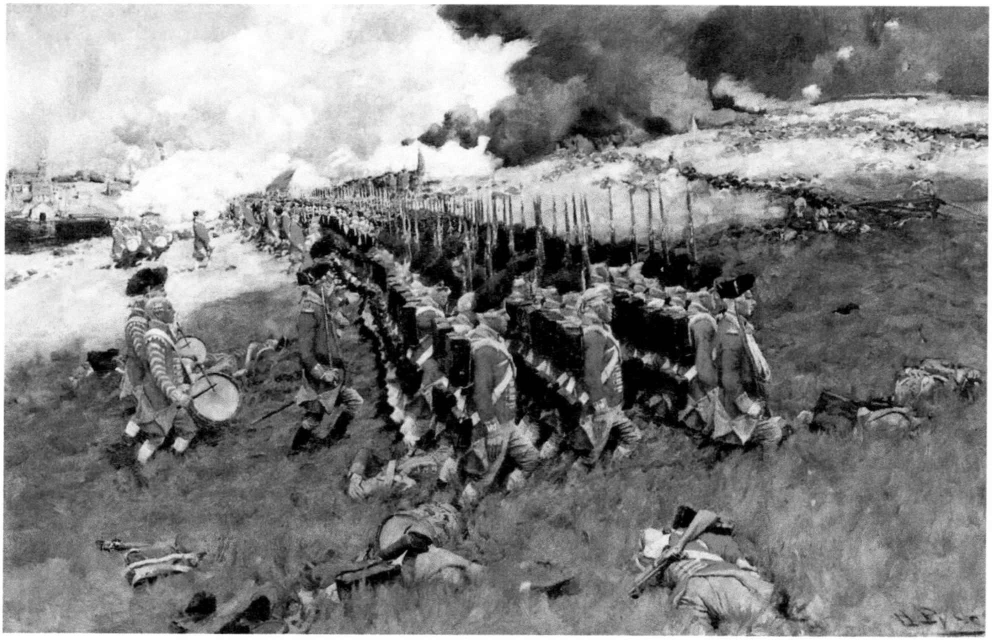

Battle of Bunker Hill, from *Scribner's Magazine*, 1898.

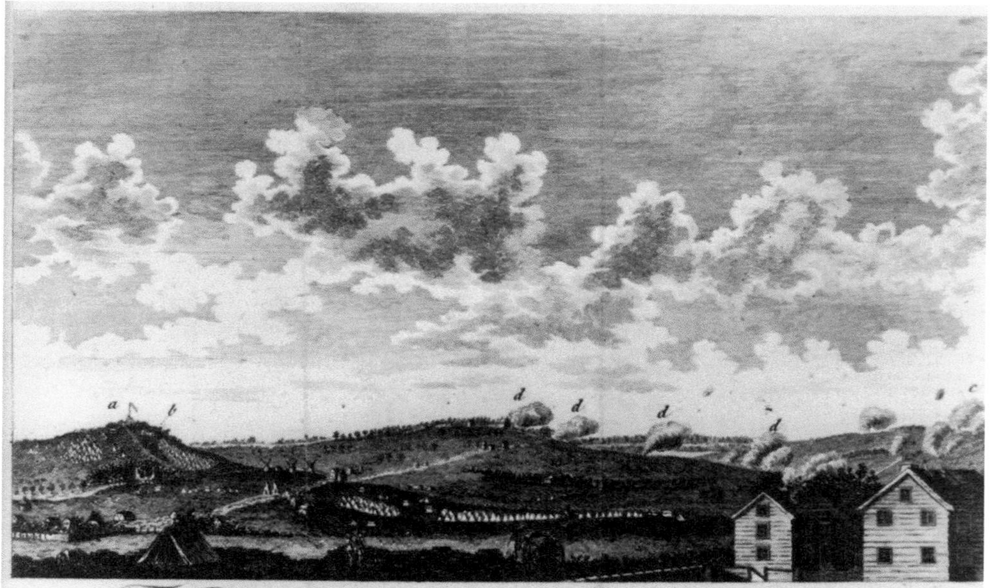

Contemporary print of the Battle of Newport, 1778. (© Library of Congress)

With the loss of the American colonies the British Empire went into a second phase of development, mainly focused on expansion in Asia and Africa. The 22nd Foot, which was officially known as the 22nd (Cheshire) Regiment of Foot by the end of the eighteenth century, played a significant role in the expansion of British influence across the Indian subcontinent in the early 1800s. At this time in its history, much of India was ruled by a vast private British company – the East India Company (EIC) – which ruled its territories in close cooperation with the British government. In 1805, the 22nd were part of an EIC force that suffered heavy casualties during the unsuccessful storming of the vast Indian fortress at Bhurtpore, in Rajasthan. The fortress proved to be virtually impregnable, and was only captured twenty years later, in 1825, by EIC forces under the command of Sir Stapleton Cotton.

In 1843, the EIC tried to expand its control into north-western India by launching an invasion of the province of Sind. A modest invasion force of 3,000 men, under Sir Charles Napier, was given the task of seizing the territory. The EIC army invading Sind contained only one British crown regiment, the 22nd Cheshire's, when it clashed with the armies of the emir rulers of Sind, at the Battle of Miani in February 1843. The Cheshire's went straight for the centre of the enemy line at Miani, then opened fire at close range. The

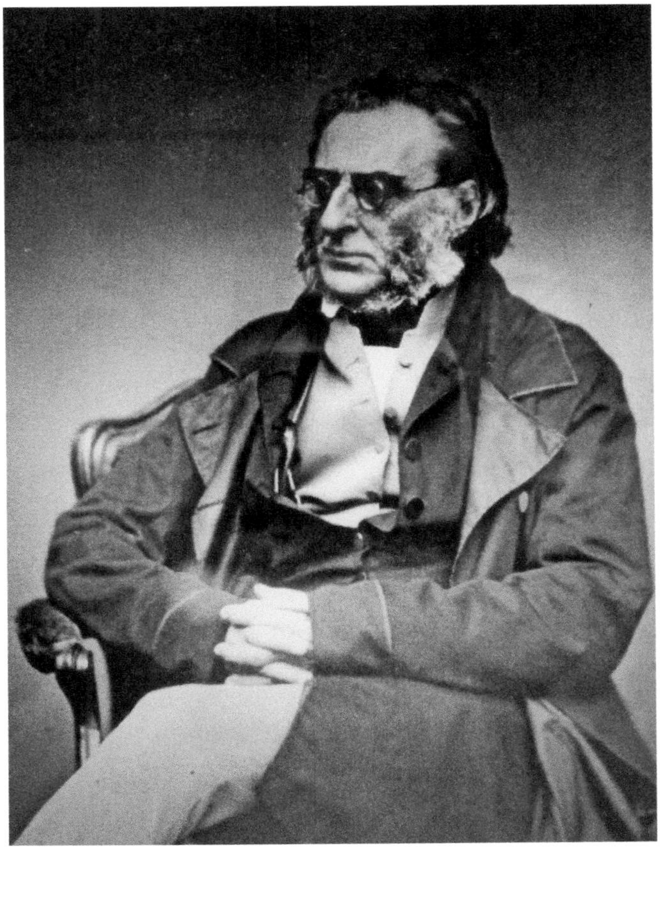

Early daguerrotype of Charles Napier, 1849.

well-directed volley fire from the British regiment, combined with a bayonet charge, broke the Indian line, and Napier was victorious. Sind was secured for the East India Company, and for the British. After the battle, legend has it that Napier sent a brief celebratory message to the EIC's governor-general, simply stating '*peccavi*' (Latin for 'I have sinned'). In reality, though, this Latin pun had nothing to do with Napier, but was instead the work of a seventeen-year-old Victorian schoolgirl called Catherine Winkworth.

The links between the 22nd Foot and its Chester origins were certainly shown in 1782, when the regiment was retitled the 22nd (Cheshire) Regiment of Foot. Even so, it took nearly a hundred years for the bond between Chester, Cheshire and the 22nd Foot to grow much closer. The Cardwell Reforms of the early 1870s, followed by the 1881 Childers Reforms, created a more locally based, regionally structured army. Regiments were required to have two battalions (one training battalion and one based overseas) and to recruit from a particular geographical area. In 1873, the 22nd Foot was given a depot at Chester Castle, and on 1 July 1881, the 22nd Foot officially became known as the Cheshire Regiment, recruiting men from around the county of Cheshire. The 22nd Foot/Cheshire Regiment survived the Cardwell and Childers Reforms largely unscathed, primarily because it was already a two-battalion regiment and didn't need amalgamation with another military formation. Indeed, the Cardwell measures led to the formation of a third battalion of the Cheshire Regiment, made up of former militia groups in the area.

Battalions of the Cheshire Regiment continued to serve in India, but by the end of the nineteenth century Britain's military focus had shifted away from Asia towards southern Africa. In particular, between 1899 and 1902 Britain became engaged in a brutal war

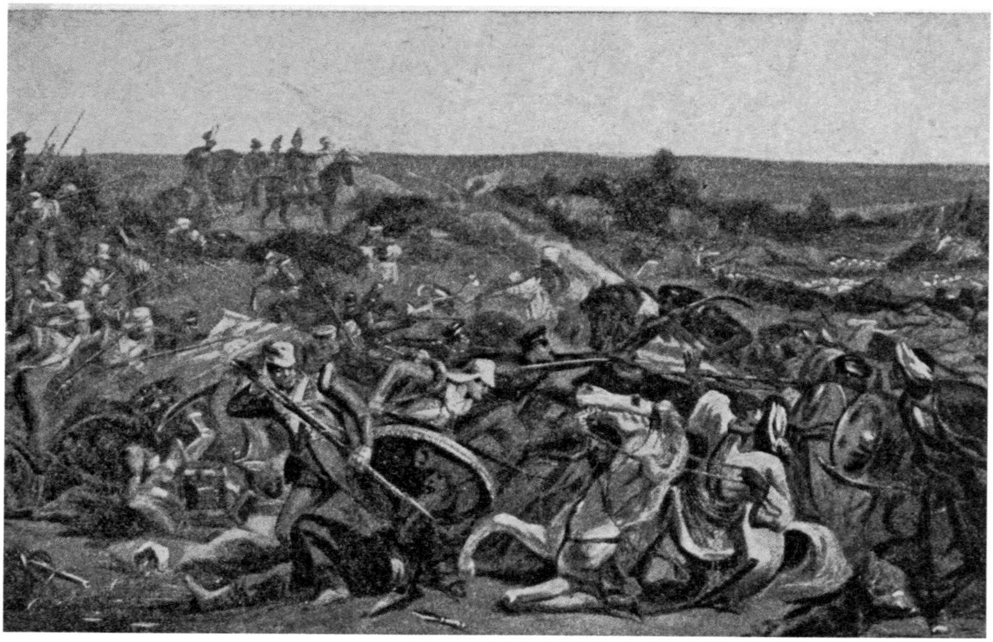

Battle of Miani, by James Bryce, *c.* 1915–20.

Foreign Affairs.

It is a common idea that the most laconic military despatch ever issued was that sent by Cæsar to the Horse-Guards at Rome, containing the three memorable words "*Veni, vidi, vici*," and, perhaps, until our own day, no like instance of brevity has been found. The despatch of Sir Charles Napier, after the capture of Scinde, to Lord Ellenborough, both for brevity and truth, is, however, far beyond it. The despatch consisted of one emphatic word—"*Peccavi*," "I have Scinde," (*sinned*).

'Peccavi', *Punch Magazine*, 18 May 1844.

against the Dutch Boer settlers of the Transvaal and the Orange Free State. A clash between the imperial-minded British, intent on extending their domains in southern Africa, and the independent Boer farmers had long been anticipated. When fighting broke out in 1899, the results proved to be calamitous for the British. The towns of Mafeking and Ladysmith were besieged by Boer forces, and British armies suffered military reverses at Spion Kop, Colenso and the Tugela River. Britain's military difficulties during the early stages of the Boer War were probably inevitable, given the fact that it had only 10,000 men immediately available to fight in the conflict. By contrast, on paper at least, the Boers could mobilise roughly 85,000 men, mostly with their own horses and accurate Mauser rifles. To be victorious in the conflict, the British had to gather their reserves from across the empire, and channel them into the fight against the Boers. Some of these reserves came from Chester, and the county of Cheshire; for example, the 2nd and 3rd battalions of the Cheshire Regiment were dispatched to fight in South Africa. The war fought by the men of the Cheshire Regiment contained few pitched battles. Instead, it was largely a guerrilla war of ambushes and sabotage. The Boers proved to be a determined, implacable enemy, and British forces resorted to burning down Boer farms and crops, and placing

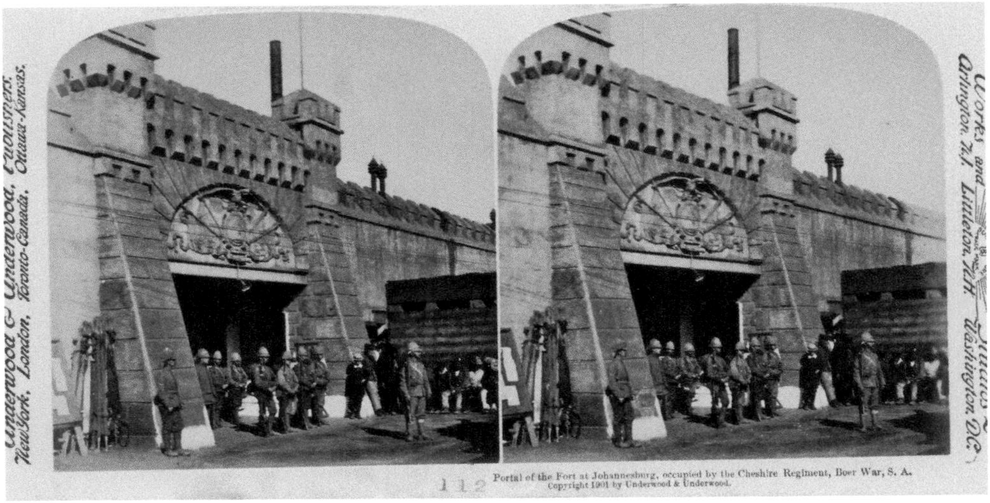

Cheshire Regiment at Johannesburg Fort, 1901. (© Rijksmuseum, Netherlands)

Boer families in what turned out to be the world's first concentration camps. Deprived of aid from their families and farms, the Boer guerrillas were really starved into submission before a final peace treaty was signed at Vereeniging in 1902. Only then could the men of the Cheshire Regiment, along with all the other forces of the empire, return home after the end of one of the largest, most controversial imperial wars of the whole Victorian era. One of the key strategic lessons learned from this war (at least as far as army planners were concerned) was that Britain had insufficient trained reserves to call upon in order to fight a major conflict. This led to a further reorganisation of Volunteer and Militia forces in 1908, in which Volunteer formations were transformed into Territorials, and Militias became Special Reserves. All this meant that the Cheshire Regiment grew in size yet further, to include one Reserve and four Territorial battalions.

Twelve years after the end of the Boer conflict, the Cheshire Regiment again went to war. The onset of the First World War, in August 1914, transformed the regiment almost beyond recognition. Between 1914 and 1918, thirty-eight battalions of men were raised under its colours (a typical battalion might contain between 600 and 1,000 men). Most of these battalions served at some stage on the Western Front in the largely static, complex series of trench lines that sprang up between the North Sea and Switzerland to the south. In fact, the Cheshire's 1st Battalion served in France and Belgium before the extensive trench systems even appeared. The battalion crossed to France at the onset of the war, in August 1914, as part of the 100,000-strong British Expeditionary Force (BEF). The German kaiser referred to this force as a 'contemptible' little army, when compared to the massive millions-strong armies of the Germans, French and Russians. The 'Old Contemptibles' as

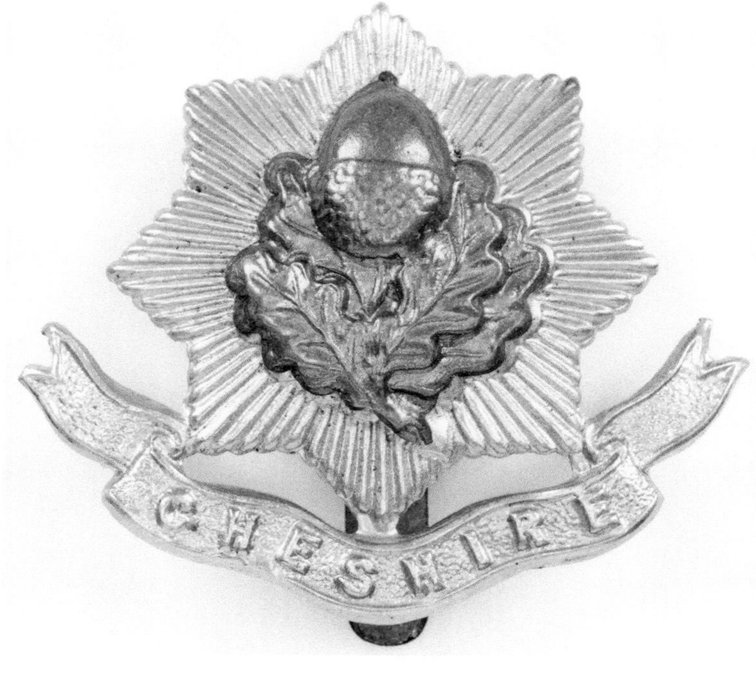

First World War Cheshire Regiment cap badge. (© Auckland Museum)

they became known, fought a series of fluid, mobile defensive battles, which eventually helped stop the German advance on Paris. Only when the German onslaught had been stopped by the French and the BEF (which was largely destroyed in the process) did the war start to degenerate into static trench warfare – from the end of 1914 onwards.

In addition to fighting in the blood-soaked campaigns of the Western Front, the Cheshire Regiment also fought in other key theatres of war around the world. In October 1915, the regiment's 2nd Battalion landed in Salonika, Greece, in order to support Serbia's struggles against the Austro-Hungarian Empire (a key ally of Germany). The Cheshire battalion became part of what was known as the Macedonian Front – a little-known theatre of war that eventually involved over 500,000 British and other Allied soldiers. This particular military venture achieved little, as did some other British attempts to undermine Turkey and the Ottoman Empire (another major ally of Germany). Units of the Cheshire Regiment were involved in fighting in Mesopotamia, along the River Tigris – in what is now modern Iraq – in a campaign that ended disastrously with British forces under General Townshend surrendering to the Turks at the town of Kut. Elements of the Cheshire Regiment also landed at Suvla Bay in the Dardanelles, in 1915, as part of the Gallipoli campaign against the Turks. The object of this campaign was to capture the Gallipoli Peninsula, so that supplies could be sent to the Russians, via sea, in order to assist them in their battles against both the Germans and the Austro-Hungarians. The Allied landings at Gallipoli, commanded by Sir Ian Hamilton, were in most respects an unmitigated disaster. Large number of British, French and ANZAC (Australian and New Zealand) troops were pinned down for months on end by the Turks, until a humiliating evacuation was ordered at the end of the year. The Cheshire Regiment was

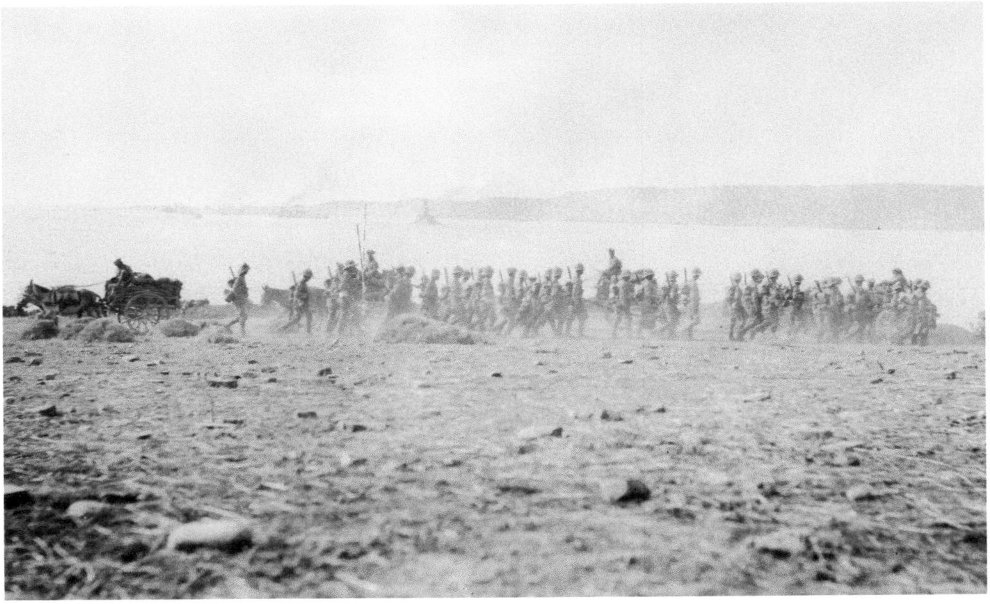

British troops at Suvla Bay, 1915. (© Alexander Turnbull Library)

also involved in the far more successful British campaigns against the Turks in Palestine and the Middle East. General Allenby took command of a British and Commonwealth army that invaded Ottoman-controlled Palestine during 1917. The regiment took part in the key battles to dislodge Turkish forces occupying a defensive line between Gaza and Beersheeba. These battles, which focused on the capture of the water wells at Beersheba, were a complete success. Large numbers of water-carrying camels supplied the Cheshire Regiment contingents, and the rest of the Allied army, and Jerusalem fell to the advancing troops on 9 December 1917.

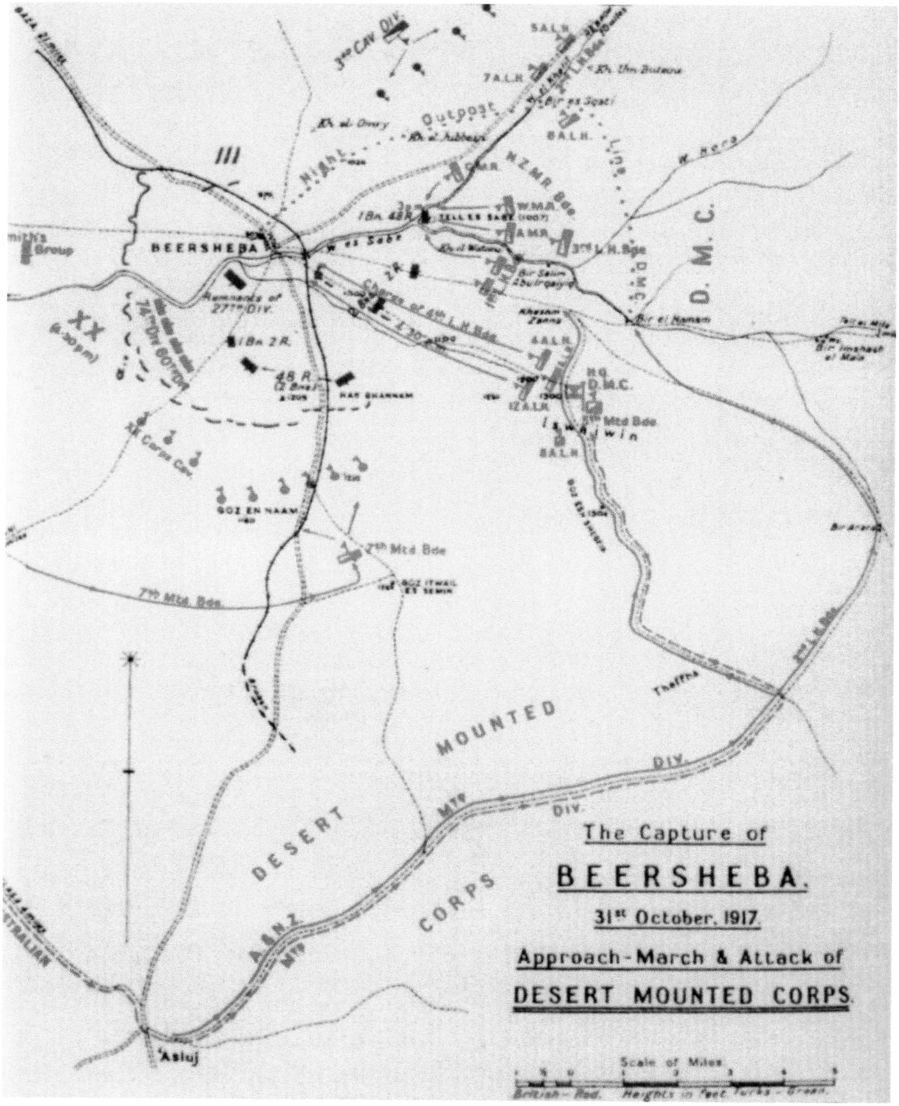

Official 1930 British government map of the Battle of Beersheba.

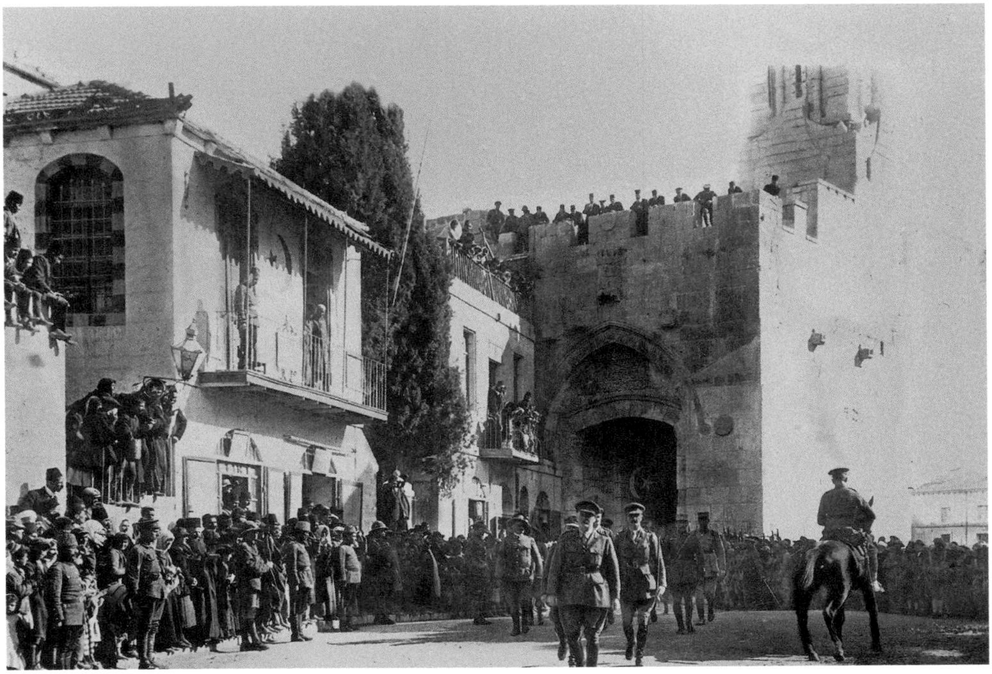

General Allenby reviewing British troops in Jerusalem, 1917. (© National Photo Collection of Israel)

Seven battalions of the Cheshire Regiment also fought in the Second World War. Three battalions (the 2nd, 4th and 7th) were part of the original BEF, which went to France at the onset of war in September 1939 and was later driven back to the beaches around Dunkirk in May/June 1940. Subsequently, the 1st, 2nd and 6th battalions were involved in Britain's long North African desert campaign against German and Italian forces, which lasted from the end of 1940 until the final surrender of all Axis forces in Tunisia, in May 1943. The 1st Battalion of the Cheshire Regiment was involved in the early stages of the campaign. In late 1940, Italian armies based in Libya attacked the British in Egypt. The 1st Cheshire's were part of the British army, which drove the Italians all the way back to Benghazi. After this, the 1st Battalion was posted to the besieged island of Malta, which, for a long period between 1941 and 1942, became the most bombed place on earth. The island bestrode the Axis powers' supply routes to North Africa. Ships supplying Rommel's Africa Corps with food, fuel and equipment could be sunk by British planes and naval forces based in Malta, and as a result the Germans and Italians did everything they could to batter the island into submission. The attempt failed, and the 1st Cheshire's left the island in 1943. By early 1945, however, the battalion was back in action in north-western Europe, when it took part in General Montgomery's last great set piece battle of the Second World War – the massive Allied military assaults across the River Rhine.

The 2nd and 6th battalions of the Cheshire Regiment also took part in the Battle of El Alamein, which proved to be the decisive turning point in the North African desert campaign. The Cheshire battalions took up position in an Allied line that stretched

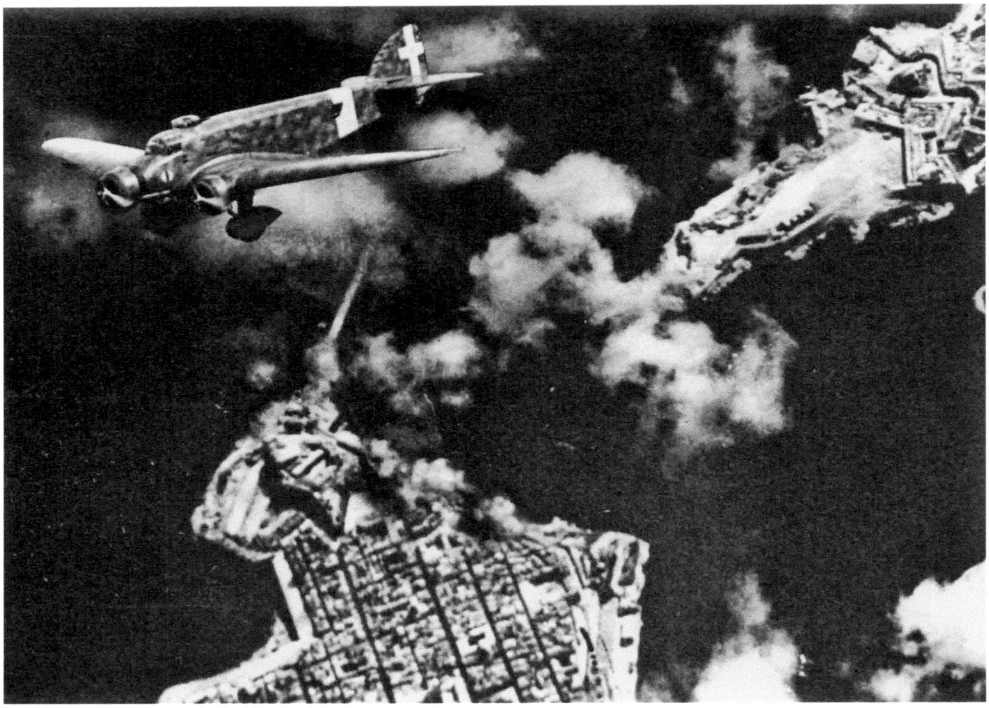

Italian plane bombing Valletta, Malta, 19 June 1941. (© Italian Central Archives)

from the impassable Qattara Depression in the south, northwards to the Mediterranean Sea, and which pivoted around a small railway station at El Alamein. On 22 October 1942, after a huge artillery bombardment, British and Allied infantry (including the Cheshire's) advanced to take on Rommel's Axis armies in a savage twelve-day battle, which ended with the complete defeat of the Germans and their allies. Once the North African coastline had been cleared of German and Italian troops, overall Allied strategy (principally supported by Churchill and the British) dictated that Italy should be invaded next. Italy was deemed to be the 'soft underbelly' through which Germany could be weakened and destroyed.

Both the 2nd and 7th battalions of the Cheshire Regiment took part in the successful Sicily landings of July 1943. After Sicily had been taken, the Cheshire's 2nd Battalion returned to England, and subsequently landed in Normandy on D-Day – 6 June 1944. The battalion then fought through the Normandy hedgerows and advanced as far as the River Waal in the Netherlands, before being recalled to England. The 7th Battalion continued to fight on in Italy, where it was joined by both the Cheshire's 6th and 8th battalions. The 8th acted principally as a guard battalion in Rome, but the 6th and 7th Cheshire's fought their way up through Italy in the face of much desperate and sustained German resistance. Any thoughts that Italy might be the 'soft underbelly' of German dominated Europe were quickly dispelled by the savagery of the fighting at Salerno, Anzio, the Gothic Line, and a whole host of other battlefields. By the time the Cheshire's had advanced into northern

Italy, in early 1945, it was clear to see (as many post-war historians pointed out) that Italy had been a 'tough old gut' rather than the soft underbelly of German-dominated Europe.

Following the end of the Second World War there was an inevitable reduction in the size of the Cheshire Regiment. The 1st and 2nd battalions were merged into one depot battalion in 1948. Following this, however, the Cheshire's were still deployed around the world for many decades, under both British and United Nations command. The period after 1945 brought about the rapid demise of the British Empire. Nationalist movements arose in many colonies and protectorates, which pushed – some of them violently – for independence from Britain. The Cheshire Regiment was one regiment among many that faced the wrath of nationalist sentiment in various postings across the soon-to-be liquidated British Empire. In 1951, the regiment was in Egypt, at a time when Arab nationalism was certainly on the rise. Between 1948 and 1960, British forces were also committed to fighting in the colony of Malaya (finally given its independence in 1957) against bands of communist insurgents led by the guerrilla leader Chin Penn. During 1957, the Cheshire Regiment participated in this campaign against Chin Penn's guerrillas, which was ultimately successful, and led to the emergence of a stable and democratic Malaysia.

The Cheshire Regiment was not just concerned with maintaining order during the post-war period of decolonisation. During the Cold War in Europe, the Cheshire's were often garrisoned in West Germany, as part of the North Atlantic Treaty Organisation

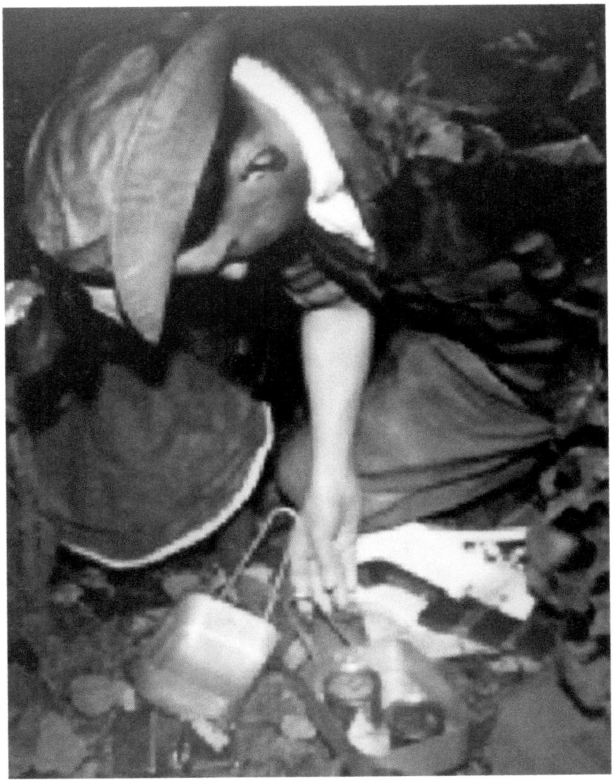

Malayan jungle tableaux with corporal brewing up by his 'basha'. (© Cheshire Military Museum)

(NATO) forces positioned to resist the massive Soviet bloc armies on the other side of the Iron Curtain.

The Cheshire Regiment has also been linked to the troubled history of Ireland for centuries, and in 1970 it was one of the first regiments to be deployed to Ulster, as part of Operation Banner – which became the longest continuous deployment of British troops in UK military history. The regiment was posted to Derry in 1970, and future postings to Ulster during the period of 'The Troubles' soon followed. In 1980, the Cheshire's became the resident regiment at Shackleton Barracks, Ballykelly, in County Derry. This particular posting led to one of the darkest days in the regiment's history: on 6 December 1982 eight of its off-duty soldiers, together with three soldiers from other regiments and six civilians (mostly teenagers), were killed by an Irish National Liberation Army (INLA) bomb while attending a pre-Christmas celebration at the Droppin Well disco venue in Ballykelly.

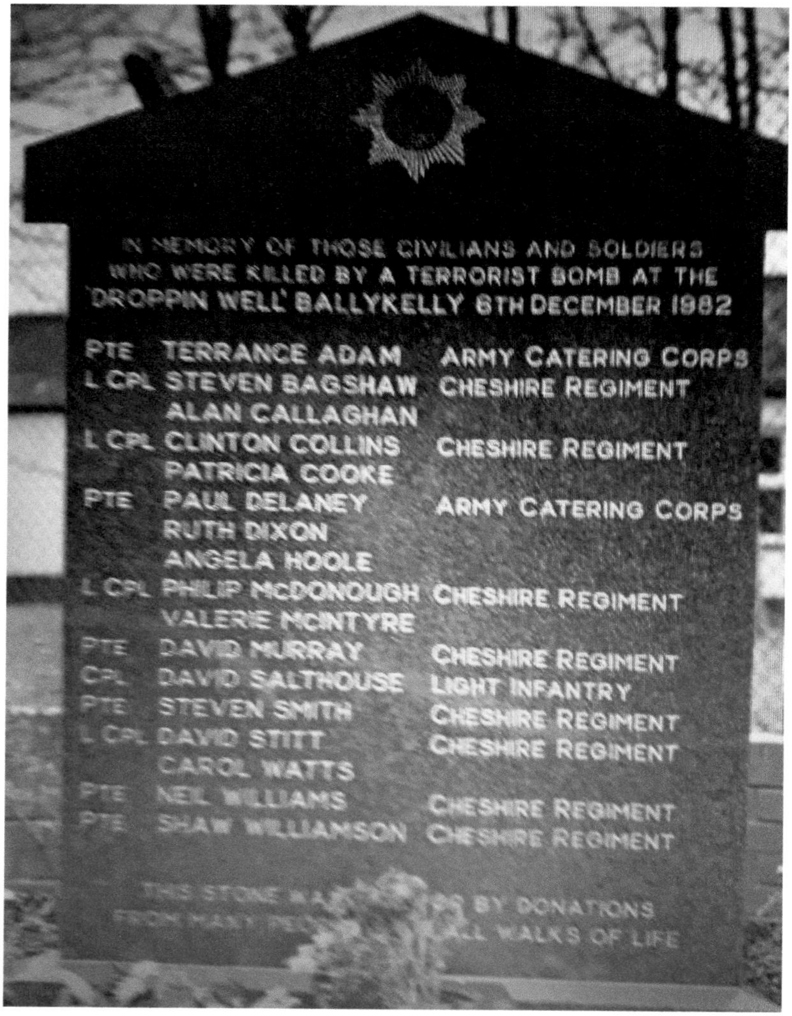

Droppin' Well Memorial, 1982. (© Cain Conflict Archive, Ulster) University

Further afield, the Cheshire Regiment found itself under United Nations command on various vital peacekeeping duties. In 1992, the regiment was posted to Bosnia, under the command of Lieutenant-Colonel Bob Stewart, where it served as part of the 7th Armoured Brigade UN force, which tried to restore peace in an area ripped apart by civil war following the disintegration of the former state of Yugoslavia.

In 2004, the Cheshire Regiment also took part in the Iraq War, again operating as part of the 7th Armoured Brigade. The Iraq War was undoubtedly controversial, in a political sense. Nevertheless, the regiment carried out its military tasks with all the professionalism and sense of duty one would expect from a body with such a long and illustrious history. The survival of the regiment as an independent entity only came under threat in comparatively recent times: in 2004, plans were made public to merge the Cheshire Regiment with the Staffordshire Regiment and the Worcestershire and Sherwood Foresters in order to create the new Mercian Regiment. In August 2007, these plans came to fruition when the former Cheshire Regiment officially became the first battalion of the Mercian Regiment. This new battalion carries with it over 300 years of Chester and Cheshire military history and tradition.

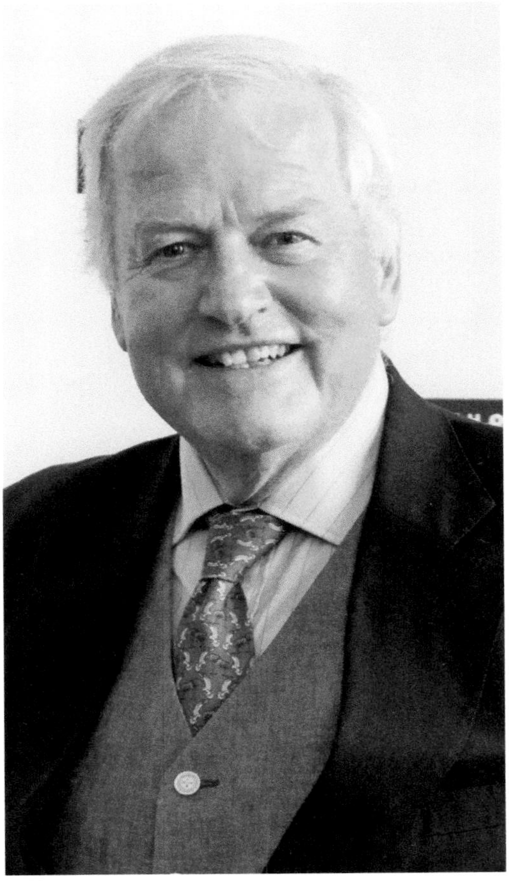

Bob Stewart, 2019. (© Bob Stewart)

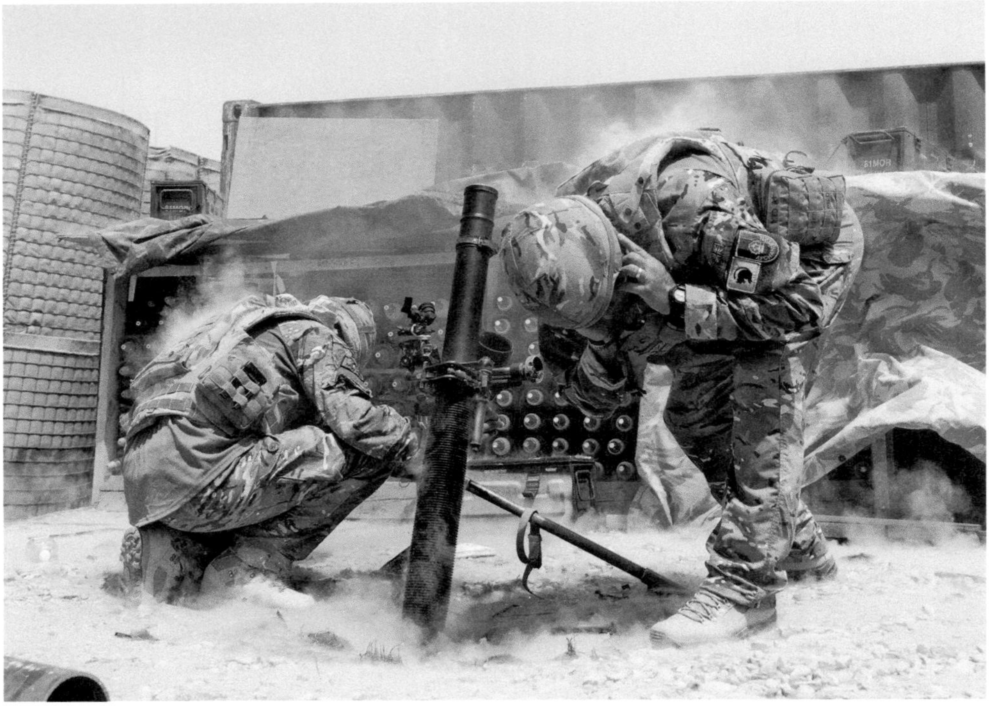

1st Battalion, Mercian (Cheshire) Regiment in action – Afghanistan, 2010, by Corporal Gary Kendall.

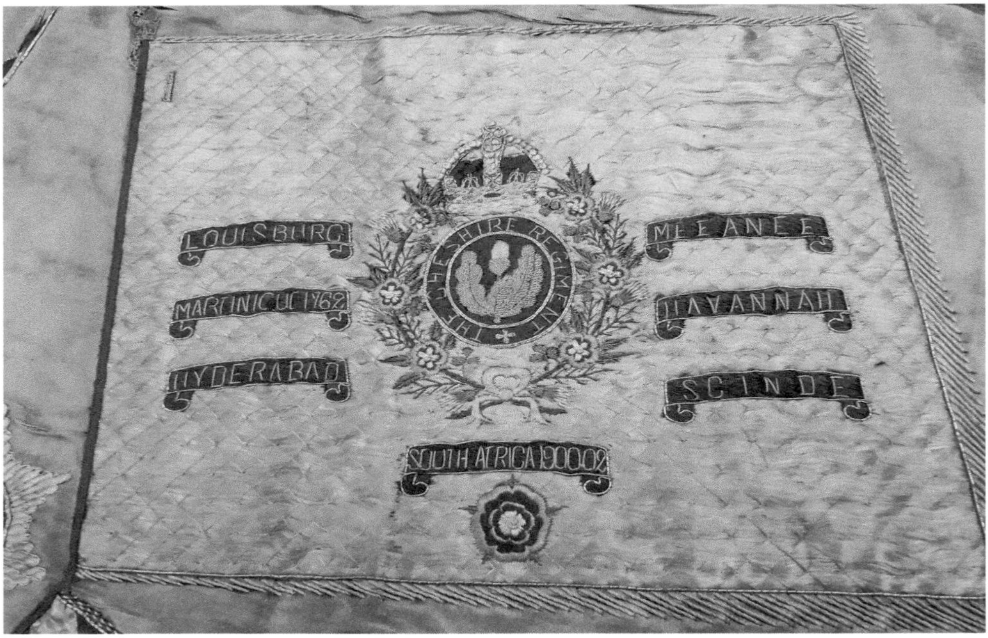

Cheshire Regiment colours, with battle honours. (© Cheshire Military Museum)

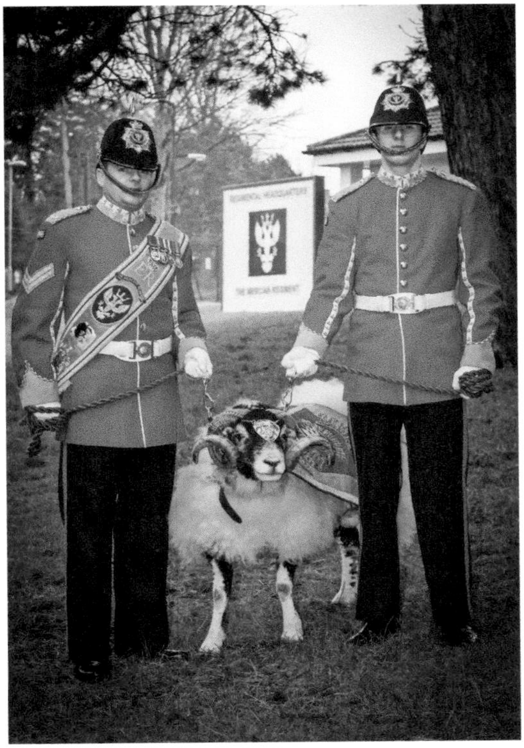

Private Derby XXX, Swaledale ram. Mercian Regiment mascot. (© Mercian Regiment)

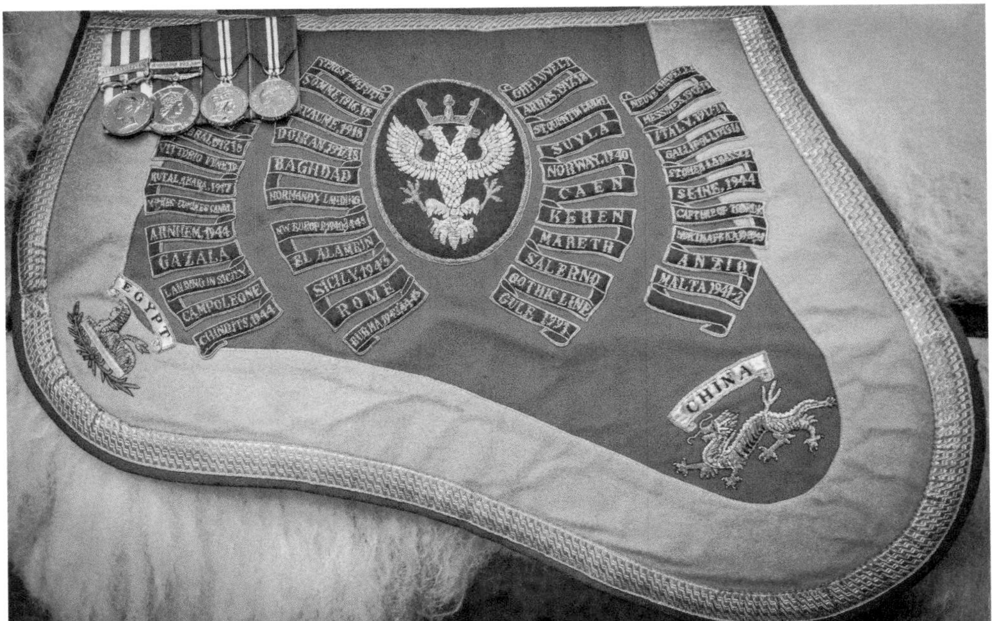

Private Derby's coat, with battle honours and medals. (© Mercian Regiment)

3. The Cheshire (Earl of Chester's) Yeomanry

The earls of Chester had ruled Chester on behalf of the monarch since the eleventh century. In 1253, the title of Earl of Chester reverted to the Crown, and from this time onwards all heirs to the crown of England numbered the earldom of Chester among their other titles and positions. In 1797 the prominent Mid Cheshire aristocrat Sir John Fleming Leicester, of Tabley House near Knutsford, secured permission from the then Prince of Wales (and future George IV) to found a new cavalry regiment called the Earl of Chester's Yeomanry (EOCY). Later, in 1803, the prince regent granted the new military unit the right to use the triple-feathered crest of the Prince of Wales as the regimental emblem. Over time, the EOCY also became known as the more general 'Cheshire Yeomanry'. This new 'citizens army' of part-time cavalrymen was very much the last word in sartorial elegance and sophistication, with uniforms modelled on the extravagant gear worn by the hussar regiments. Fleming funded the establishment of the EOCY in its

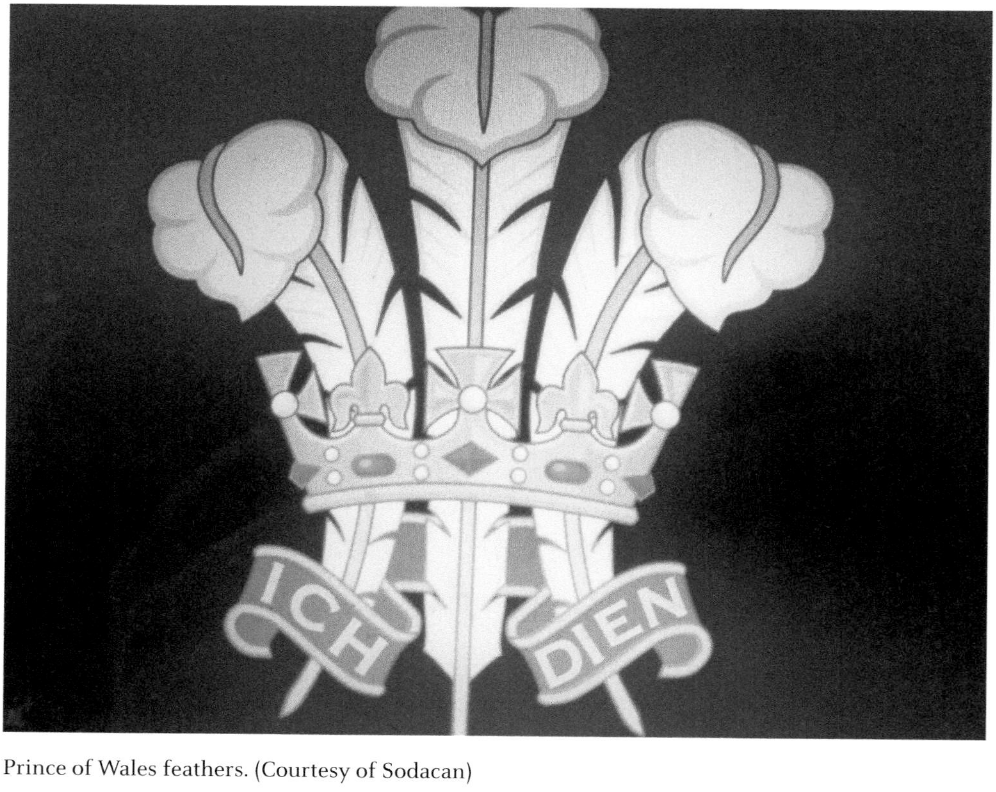

Prince of Wales feathers. (Courtesy of Sodacan)

entirety, and he and its other early leaders dressed flamboyantly in the latest fashions of the time. The new cavalry formation, centred at Chester, but with detachments at Altrincham, Northwich, Macclesfield and other key locations, was formed to meet the perceived threat of invasion from Revolutionary France, and was never intended for service overseas. During its early days, the regiment was very much the plaything of Fleming and its other leaders, and the line between social and military activities was often a blurred one. The regiment had extremely close links with the Tarporley Hunt, and its ordinary recruits were often made up of tenant farmers whose landlords were either members of the Hunt or commanding officers in the new yeomanry force. As a result, the rank-and-file cavalrymen had access to horses and could secure time off to participate in military exercises and manoeuvres. Collecting works of art, along with the costs of financing the EOCY, virtually bankrupted John Fleming Leicester. Nevertheless, other men from prominent Cheshire families such as the Grosvenors and the Egertons also became leading figures in the new cavalry regiment.

During the early nineteenth century, prior to the establishment of an independent Cheshire police force, one of the prime functions of the yeomanry force led by the Leicesters and others was to act in support of the civil powers. In the context of the 1820s and 1830s, which were times of great political and social unrest in many parts of the country, this meant that the EOCY was sometimes used by Cheshire magistrates to police

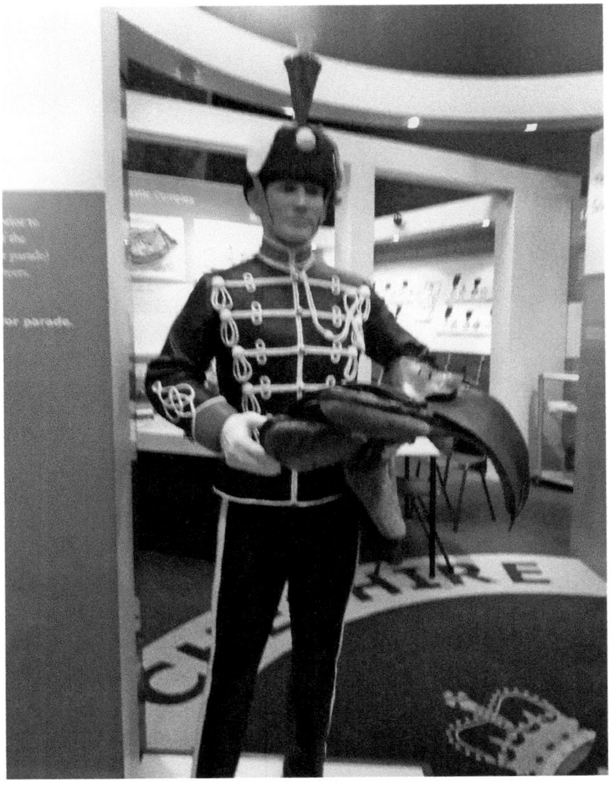

EOCY dress uniform *c*. 1890. (© Cheshire Military Museum)

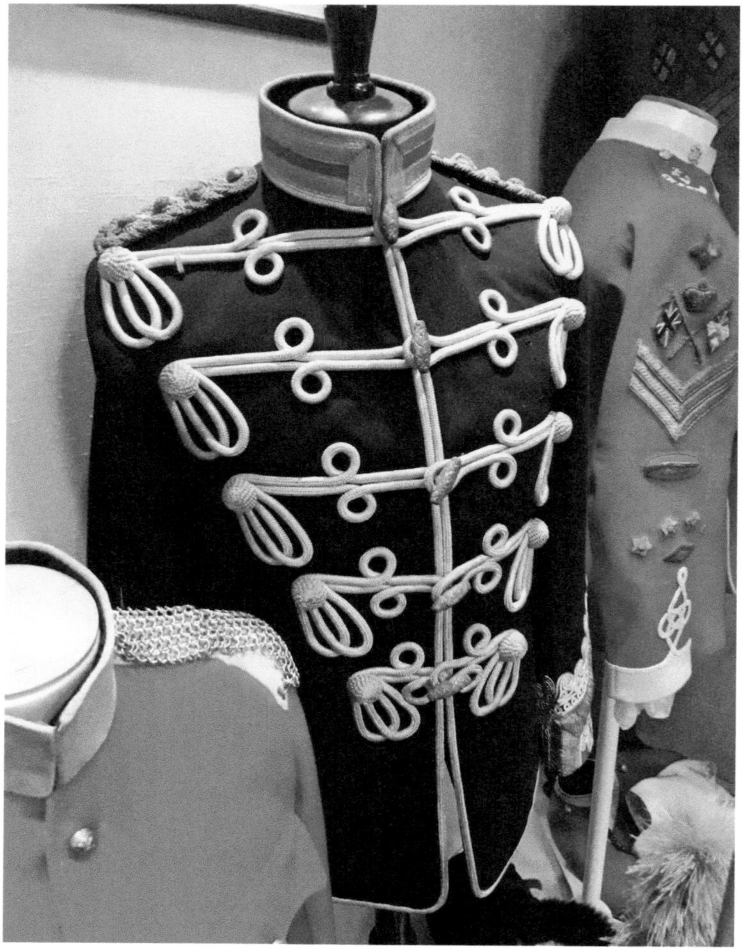

EOCY dress tunic *c.* 1890. (© Cheshire Military Museum)

and control large meetings calling for political reform and an extension of the electoral franchise. Thus, the EOCY was part of the overall yeomanry force used in the savage repression of the huge but peaceful 1819 Peterloo gathering in Manchester. Elsewhere in the county, however, detachments of the EOCY were used to enforce order with more efficiency and humanity than was shown at St Peter's Fields. In 1824, for example, riots in Macclesfield were diffused with considerable skill and diplomacy by the EOCY's adjutant, Joseph Barra. Other disturbances in Congleton and Middlewich were also policed by the regiment during this period. As the nineteenth century progressed, the maintenance of civil order became less of a priority for the yeomanry.

A number of yeomanry formations across the country struggled to survive, but for the EOCY the advent of the Boer War (1899–1902) provided new opportunities for expansion and development. In order to defeat the tough, resilient Boers of the Transvaal and the Orange Free State, the British needed greater manpower. As a result, on Christmas Eve 1899, a royal warrant was issued that requested yeomanry formations across the country

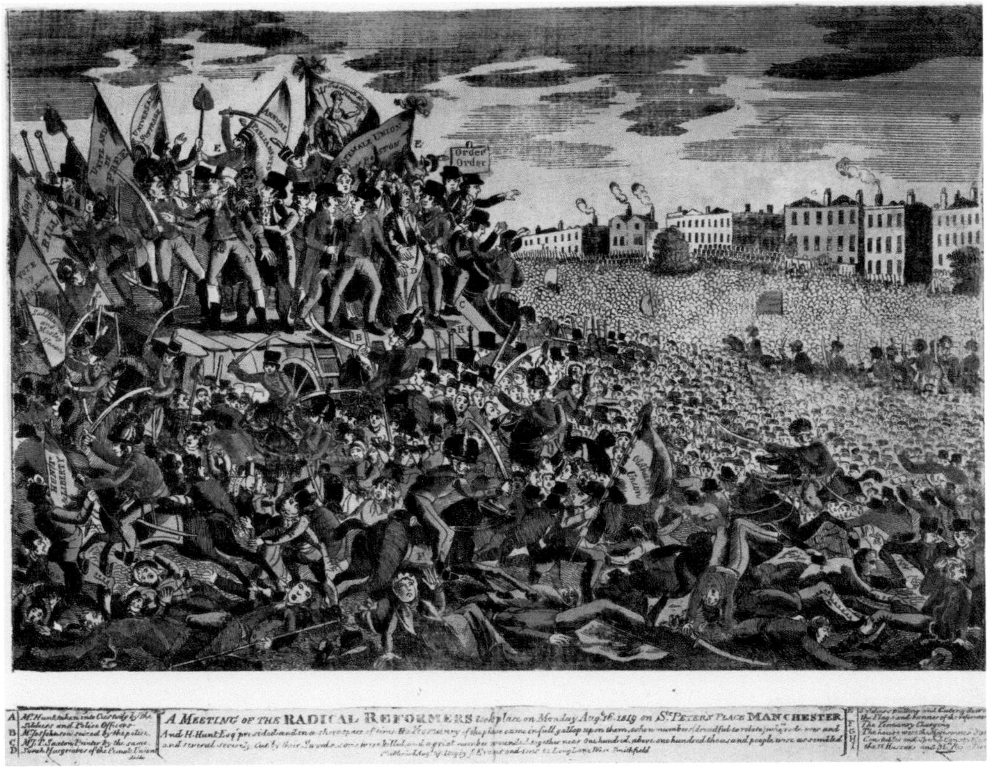

An 1819 print of the Peterloo Massacre, author unknown.

to send companies of 115 men to fight against the Boers. Yeomanry companies sent to South Africa eventually fought in what was called the Imperial Yeomanry, and from its headquarters in the Old Bank Buildings, Foregate Street, Chester, the EOCY sent two companies of men to join this new military grouping.

Although the EOCY fought in South Africa between 1899 and 1902, the overall arrangements for the disposition of yeomanry forces in the event of a future war changed yet again as a result of the 1907 Territorial and Reserve Forces Act. Under the terms of this Act, all yeomanry units were merged into a new Territorial Force intended for home service within the UK. As a result, from this date onwards no yeoman could be compelled to serve overseas. They could, instead, volunteer for what was called 'Imperial Service' in defence of the interests of the British Empire. The implications of the 1907 Act could be seen in the arrangements made for the disposition of yeomanry forces during the First World War. During the first two months of the war (August and September 1914) Territorial Force yeomen were split into different tiers. The first tier of the yeomanry was liable for service overseas, while the second tier – composed of those unable or unwilling to serve overseas – was earmarked for home service. A third line acted as a reserve, supplying replacements to the first and second tiers of the yeomanry.

The various tiers of the EOCY underwent very different experiences during the course of the First World War. The first tier was posted to Egypt in 1916 and spent most of the war participating in Allenby's successful Middle Eastern campaigns, before returning to fight on the Western Front in May 1918. At the Battle of Beersheba in 1917, and subsequently in Flanders, the Cheshire Yeomanry fought as part of the 74th (Yeomanry) Division, under the command of Major General Eric Girdwood. The second tier of the Cheshire Yeomanry was formed in 1914 and spent most of the war based in Northumberland. While in the north-east, these particular Chester cavalrymen were converted into cyclists and became part of the 6th and 10th Cyclist Brigades. Early in 1918, these newly trained cyclist soldiers were moved to the Curragh Barracks in Ireland. The Cheshire Yeomanry's third tier (formed in 1915) was also linked to the Curragh, until it was attached to the West Lancashire Division and disbanded after only two years in 1917.

Within a few years of the end of the First World War, most British cavalry regiments had been converted to other purposes. In 1921, all but the fourteen most senior cavalry formations were formed into either Signals or Armoured Car Companies. The EOCY,

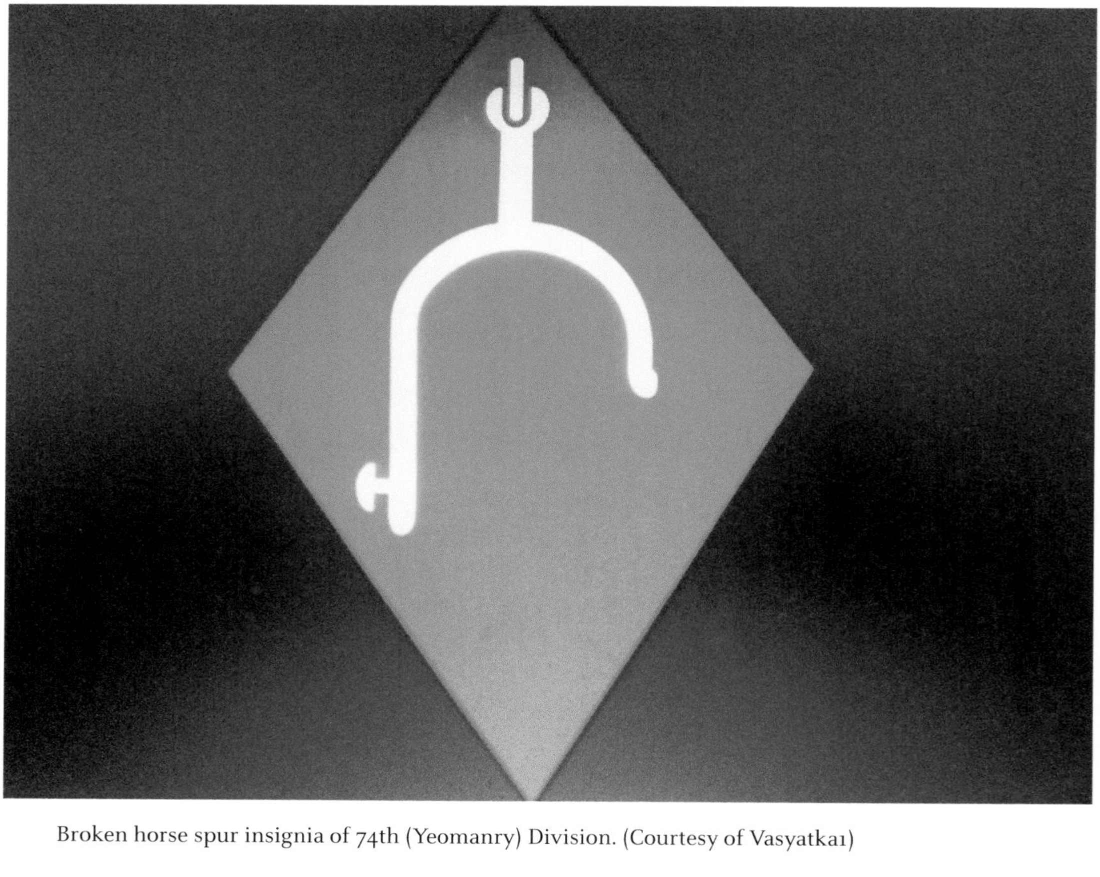

Broken horse spur insignia of 74th (Yeomanry) Division. (Courtesy of Vasyatka1)

however, (being the eighth most senior yeomanry cavalry unit in the British Army List of 1914) survived on horseback until well into the Second World War.

In 1940, at the start of the Second World War, the EOCY crossed into both Syria and Lebanon as part of a British-led invasion force intent on ensuring the removal of Vichy French power from both countries. France had dominated both Syria and Lebanon since the collapse of the Ottoman Empire at the end of the First World War. However, after France surrendered to Hitler's Germany in June 1940, a collaborationist 'puppet' French regime was set up at Vichy, under Marshall Petain. The Cheshire Yeomanry was part of an Allied army sent to ensure that the Vichy government, and the Nazis, did not establish a Syrian and Lebanese foothold in the strategically vital Middle East. The military operation was a successful one, and the Cheshire Yeomanry played its part in securing victory. The hills and plains of Syria and Lebanon were ideal terrain for cavalry, and the Cheshire Yeomanry became one of the very last cavalry regiments to fight through a campaign on horseback (until it was transformed into the mechanised 5th Line of Communications Signals Regiment in 1942).

Further changes to the EOCY were also imposed during the post-war period. In 1947, for example, it was reformed as an armoured formation, using Cromwell and Comet tanks. Twenty years later, in 1967, most of the Cheshire Yeomanry was disbanded as the result of a cost-cutting defence review. Nevertheless, residual elements of the EOCY still survived, to be formed into the Queen's Own Yeomanry in 1971, which in turn became part of the Royal Mercian and Lancastrian Yeomanry in 1999. The EOCY

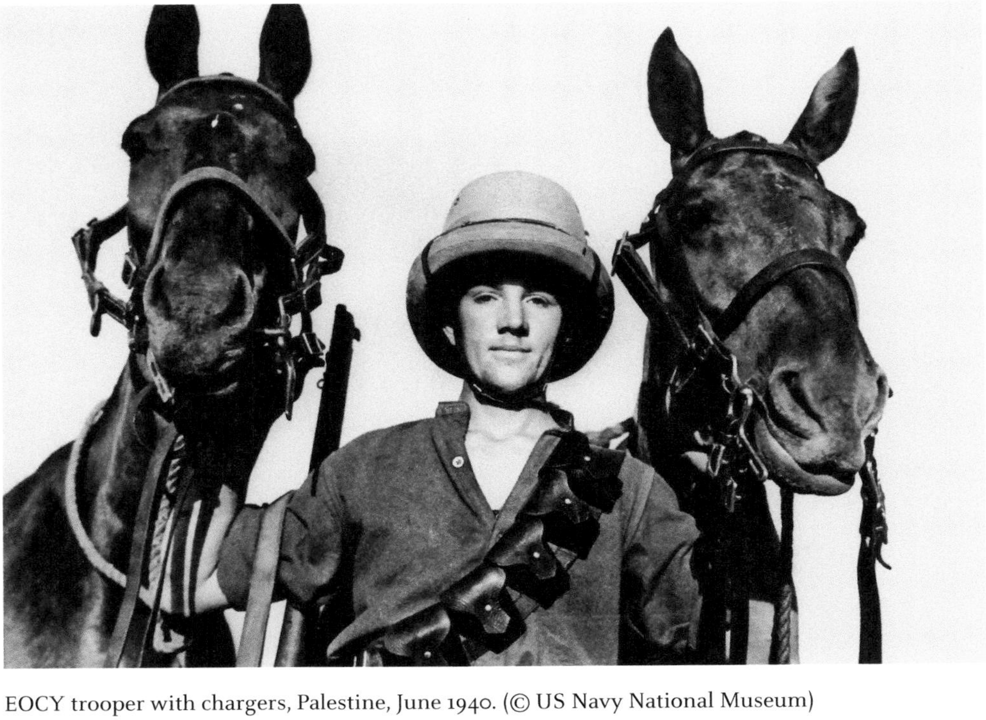

EOCY trooper with chargers, Palestine, June 1940. (© US Navy National Museum)

survives right into the twenty-first century, though in nothing like its former scale and grandeur. In 2014, C Squadron (Cheshire Yeomanry) was still based in Chester, as part of a reformed Queen's Own Yeomanry. A second squadron also continues as the 80th (Cheshire Yeomanry) Signal Squadron, which is part of 33 Signal Regiment, Royal Signals.

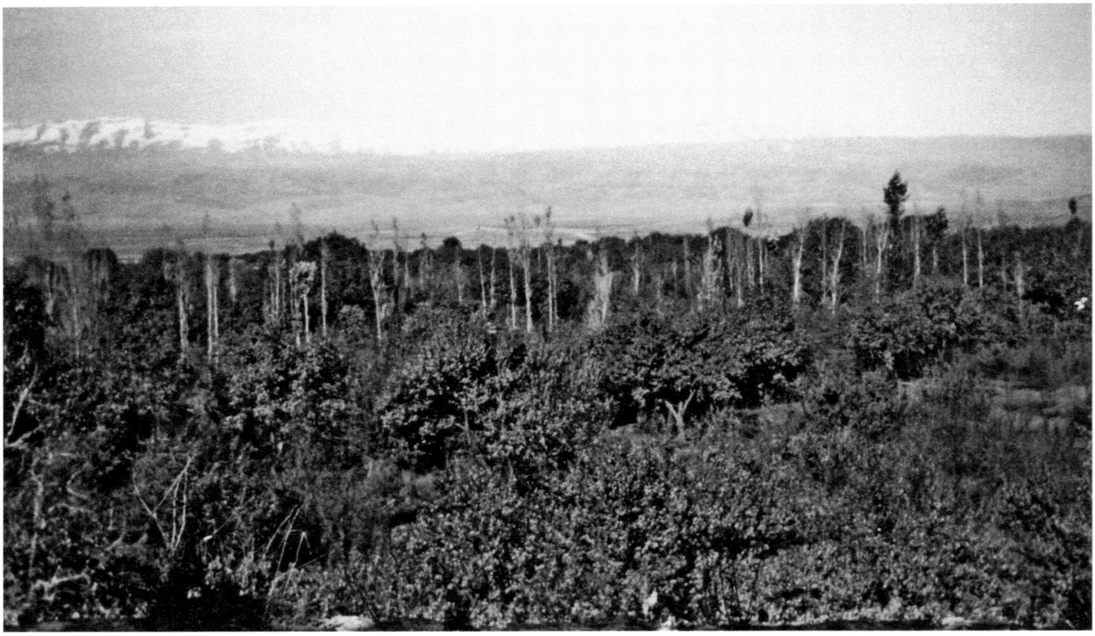

Cavalry country: Lebanon and Syria in the early 1940s. (© Tom Beazley)

4. Ceres Rising in a Winged Chariot

The Latin motto of 610 County of Chester Royal Auxiliary Air Force Squadron (RAuxAF), formed on 10 February 1936, was '*Alifero tollitur axe ceres*', which translates into English as 'Ceres rising in a winged chariot'. This motto is itself strongly indicative of the link between Chester and 610 Squadron. Ceres was the Roman goddess of agriculture and, of course, the city of Chester has a strong and rich Roman heritage. The reference to Ceres also links well with the historical importance of corn grinding in the mills along the River Dee, and with the significance of agricultural production in the hinterland of Chester. The new squadron's badge also contained the image of a sheaf of wheat, which is replicated in the armorial bearings of the city of Chester.

610 Squadron was formed at Hooton Park, near Ellesmere Port, which is less than 10 miles to the north of central Chester. As such, the bulk of 610's new recruits came from the west Cheshire and Chester area. These peacetime recruits were all part-timers, who were keen to spend their spare time and weekends flying and practising combat tactics. In general, these part-timers were of a high standard, often with previous RAF flying experience and occasionally with some involvement in the local aviation industry (the de Havilland aircraft factory, for example, was based at nearby Broughton). Auxiliary Air Force members were also seen to be a rather exclusive social group, with a more relaxed attitude to dress and discipline. Even the best pilots were sometimes not given the chance of joining the peacetime Auxiliary Air Force. James Edgar 'Johnnie' Johnson, who became a famous RAF fighter ace during the Second World War, trained at RAF Sealand and Hawarden, near Chester. He also later fought alongside 610 Squadron as part of Douglas Bader's famous Tangmere Wing, based in Sussex, and actually led the squadron between July 1942 and March 1943. Even so, Johnson wasn't judged to be suitable for the Auxiliaries, and he gained entry to the RAF via the alternative RAF Volunteer Reserve career structure.

Despite its social exclusivity, the squadron still flew some suspect machines during its early peacetime days. Prior to 1939, 610 Squadron was equipped with semi-obsolete Hawker Hind and Hawker Hart biplane light bombers. However, at the beginning of 1939, 610 was converted into a fighter squadron, and its pilots received the latest Hawker Hurricane and then Supermarine Spitfire planes during September 1939.

County of Chester 610 Squadron, RAuxAF, subsequently played a long and very distinguished role in the air battles of the Second World War. The squadron was really in the eye of the storm during the Battle of Britain, when it was based at Gravesend and then at RAF Biggin Hill in Kent. In July 1940, the squadron had twenty pilots 'on state' who were fit and ready to fight the Luftwaffe's attempts at establishing air superiority over south-eastern England. During the following two months, nine squadron pilots were killed in dog fights over London and the Home Counties, and six were badly injured. This

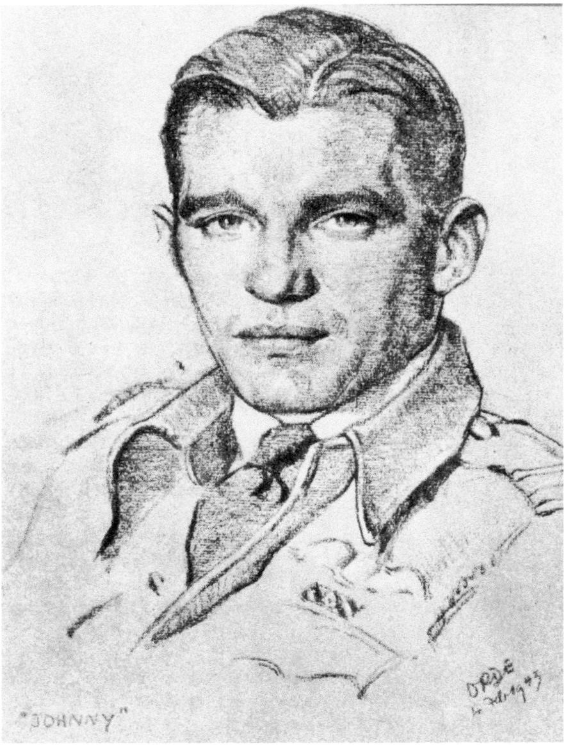

Johnnie Johnson by Cuthbert Orde, 1943.

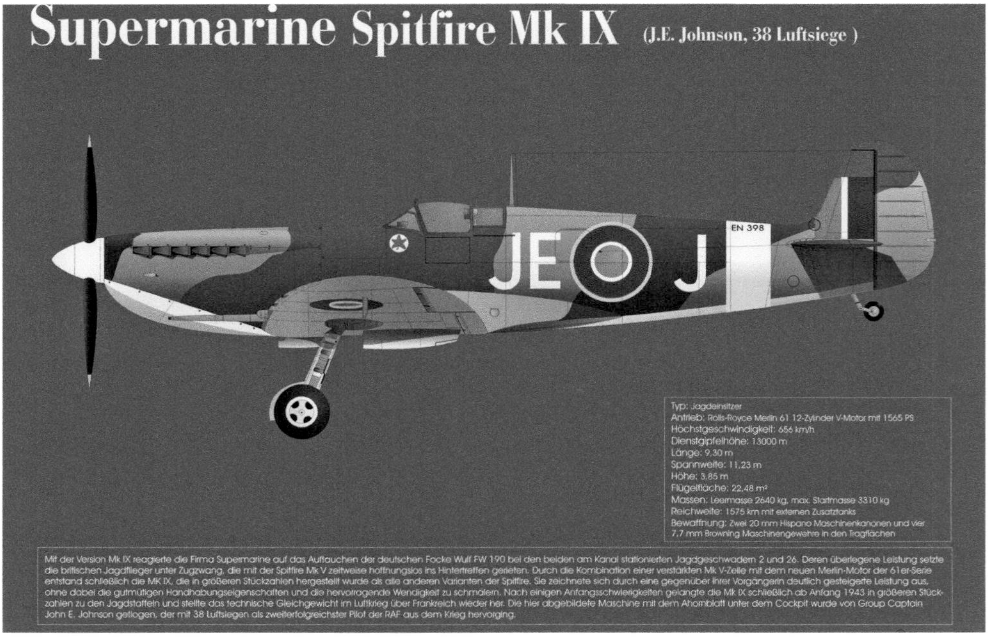

Spitfire Mk IX, 610 Squadron, with Johnnie Johnson's markings. (Courtesy of B. Huber)

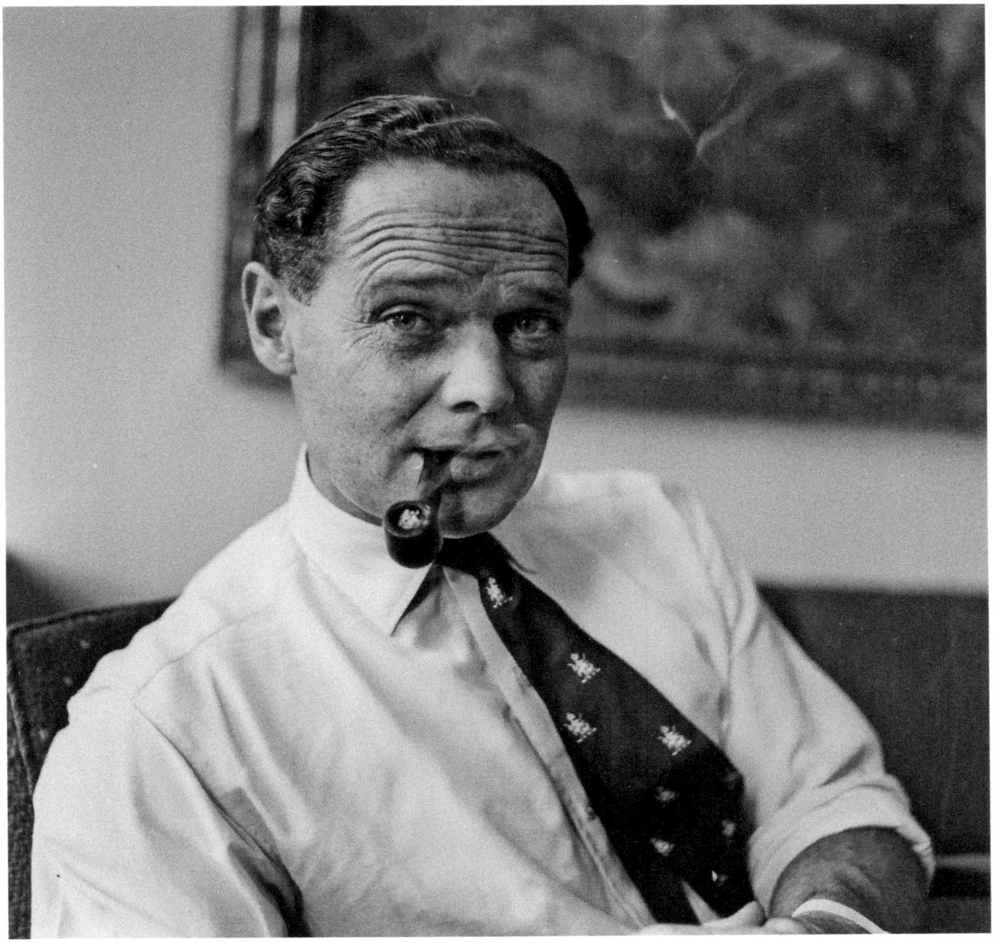

Douglas Bader, 1955. (© Archives of Norway)

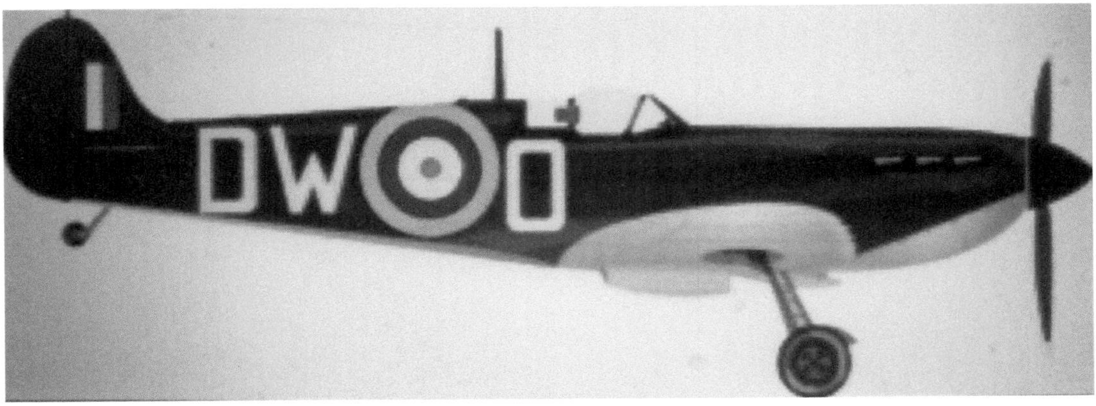

Spitfire Mk I with County of Chester markings. (Courtesy of Afromac)

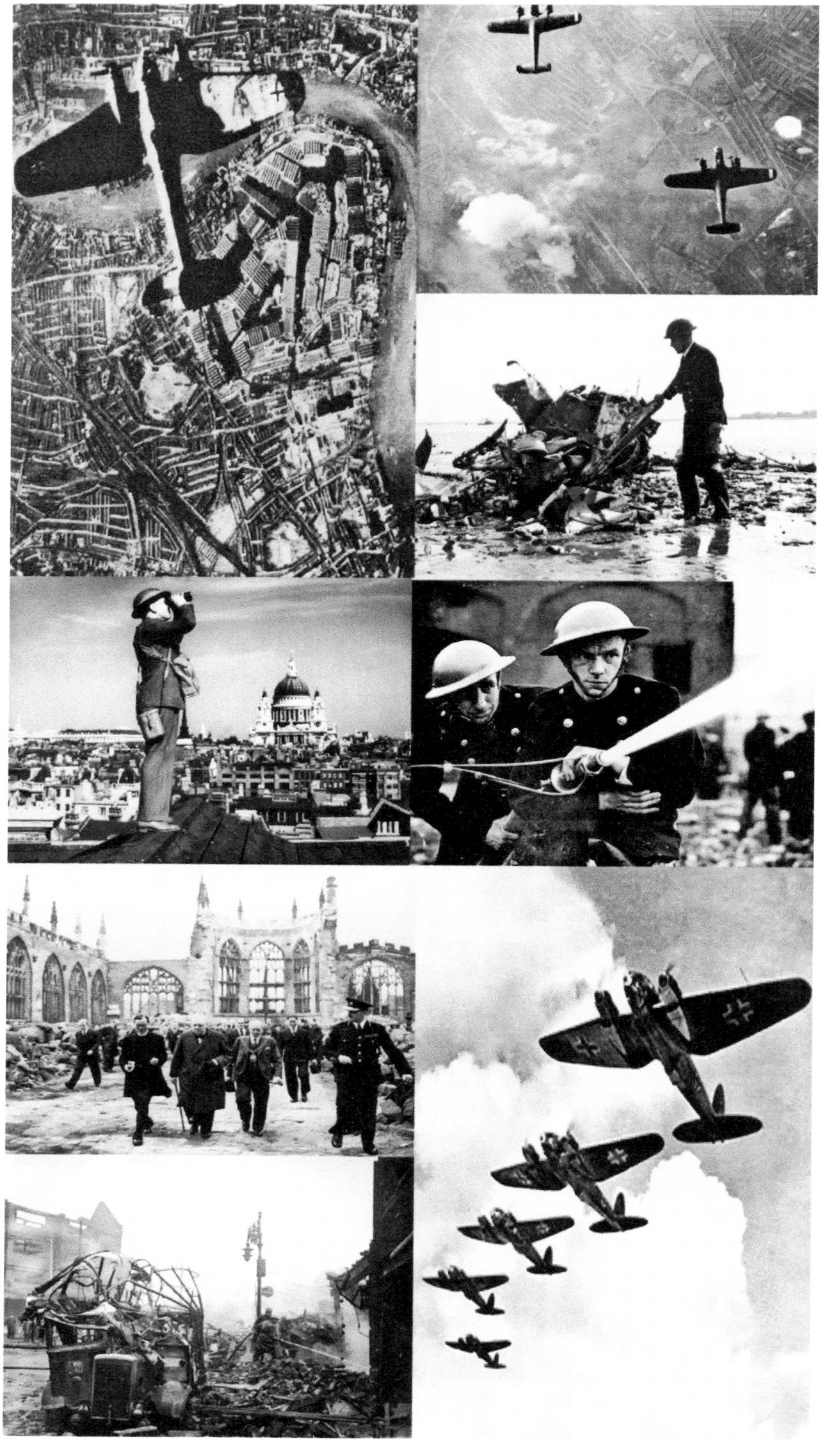

Battle of Britain collage. (© Estados Unidos de America del Sur)

represented a staggering casualty rate of 75 per cent, and predictably led to the squadron being pulled out of the front line, temporarily, at the end of August and sent to RAF Acklington in Northumberland for some much-needed rest and recuperation.

The squadron returned to the front line of the air war in 1941, when it was transferred to RAF Tangmere in Sussex, and became part of the famous Tangmere Wing commanded by the legless RAF war hero, Douglas Bader. 610 Squadron was one of three Spitfire squadrons operating from Tangmere that flew rodeo (seek and destroy) missions against German targets in north-western Europe. The Wing also flew on countless 'rhubarbs', which were defined as missions against German targets of opportunity such as airfields, road transport, trains and river traffic. 610 Squadron was based in the UK until early 1945, when it was transferred to the Continent in order to provide fighter cover for Allied armies advancing into Germany. The squadron was disbanded (temporarily) in March 1945, having shot down a total of 132 enemy aircraft and fifty V-1 flying bombs during the period of its wartime service. 610 County of Chester Squadron had fought throughout the war with considerable distinction, and it was no surprise that the successful air unit was reformed at Hooton Park in 1946 in order to help Britain meet the military and strategic challenges of the post-war world. The County of Chester Squadron entered the jet age in July 1951, when its pilots were equipped with Gloster Meteor jet fighters for the first time, and the formation continued as a front-line part of the overall RAF establishment until its final disbandment (along with all other national RAuxAF flying units) in March 1957.

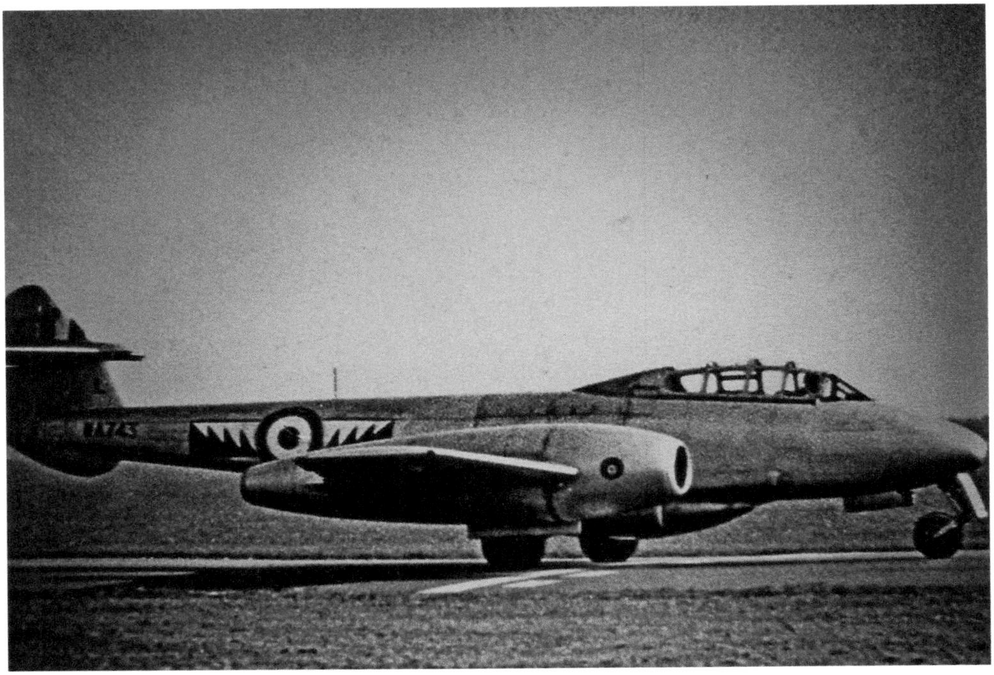

610 Squadron Gloster Meteor jet at Manchester Ringway airport, 1953. (Courtesy of RuthAS)

5. Front-line Chester

The infantry, yeomanry and air units formed in the Chester area were dispatched to fight in wars around the globe. However, over the course of many centuries, the city of Chester itself was at the centre of much military conflict. Battles were fought in its streets or within sight of the city walls. Military plots and conspiracies that involved the city were also hatched, and during the twentieth century the Chester 'home front' contributed much of value to the national war effort during two world wars. During the Second World War, in particular, Chester was in many respects a front-line city: soldiers from many nations crowded its streets, fighter aircraft and bomber planes crossed its skies, and incendiaries and other explosives were dropped on its buildings and citizens.

During the so-called Dark Ages, after the departure of the Romans from Britain, the former Roman settlement of Deva was in the front line of a struggle for dominance between Saxon invaders in the east and the native British Celtic tribes of Wales. These Celtic tribes were beginning to dominate the western fringes of Britain, linking Wales with the northern kingdom of Strathclyde. In the early years of the seventh century (probably between CE 613 and 615) Aethelfrith, the Saxon king of Northumbria, struck westwards against these Celtic forces and clashed with the combined armies of Gwynedd, and parts of Powys, at the Battle of Chester. The precise location of this battle is unclear, though in 2004 some mass graves were excavated at Heronbridge, just south of Chester, which suggest that this might have been the site of the climactic struggle between Celts and Saxons. The Battle of Chester was an emphatic, if controversial, victory for Aethelfrith's Saxons, who massacred a large number of monks from Bangor-on-Dee during the course of the fighting. The exact significance of the Saxon victory is unclear, because Aethelfrith was killed in another battle shortly afterwards. Even so, in broad strategic terms, Aethelfrith's triumph probably helped ensure that Chester's future lay within the Saxon rather than the Celtic sphere of influence.

Saxon dominance of Chester was confirmed yet again nearly 300 years later, in CE 907, when Queen Aethelflaed and her Mercians – aided and abetted by the city's inhabitants – defeated Danish attempts at taking over the settlement. Saxon dominance in Chester, and the rest of England, came to an end with the Norman Conquest of 1066, and by 1069 Hugh Lupus, Earl of Chester, was overseeing the construction of Chester's first wooden motte-and-bailey castle. This castle was used to assert control over the local population and consisted of a raised earthwork called a motte (still visible in Chester today) on which the actual castle fortifications were built. This motte was then surrounded by an enclosed bailey or courtyard, which was in turn protected by a ditch or moat. The wooden castle was being built in Chester at a time when William the Conqueror was burning crops and villages, and slaughtering the inhabitants of Yorkshire, Northumberland and elsewhere, during his so-called 'Harrying of the North'. This Norman campaign to suppress rebellion

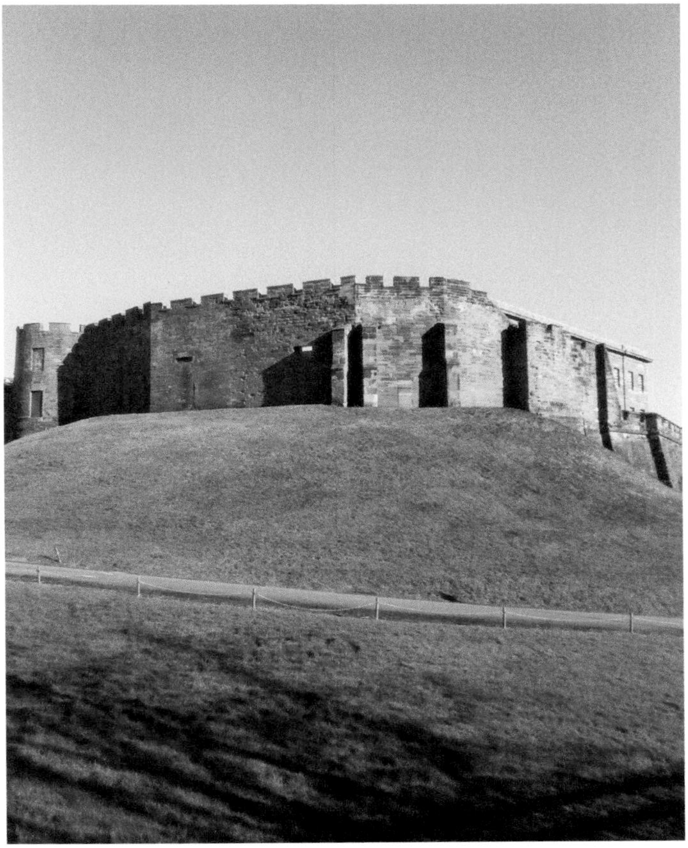

Chester Castle with original motte defence visible.

and disaffection throughout the north may well have spread to Chester in 1069–70, judging from the declining numbers of families paying land taxes. In 1066, there were around 487 homes in Chester paying Saxon land taxes (or geld). By 1086, this number had declined to 282 homes, very possibly as a result of the depredations wrought by the Norman military in the area.

Although military forces and supplies passed through Chester (on the way to either Wales or Ireland) at various points during the medieval and Tudor periods, it was not until the mid-seventeenth century that the city was again at the centre of armed conflict. During the mid-1640s, Chester was a crucial bastion of Royalist power during the English Civil War. In order to protect it, Royalist forces strengthened the city's Roman and medieval walls, and constructed an outer ring of defensive earthworks during the period 1642–43. During 1645, a complex and undulating battle for control of Chester ensued between the besieging Parliamentary forces of Colonel Michael Jones and the defending Royalists commanded by Lord Byron. In February 1645, Parliamentary assaults on the Northgate area were launched. These attacks were beaten off, and a Royalist army under Prince Maurice of Nassau (a nephew of Charles I) entered Chester to help fend off the Parliamentarians. However, Maurice left Chester during April,

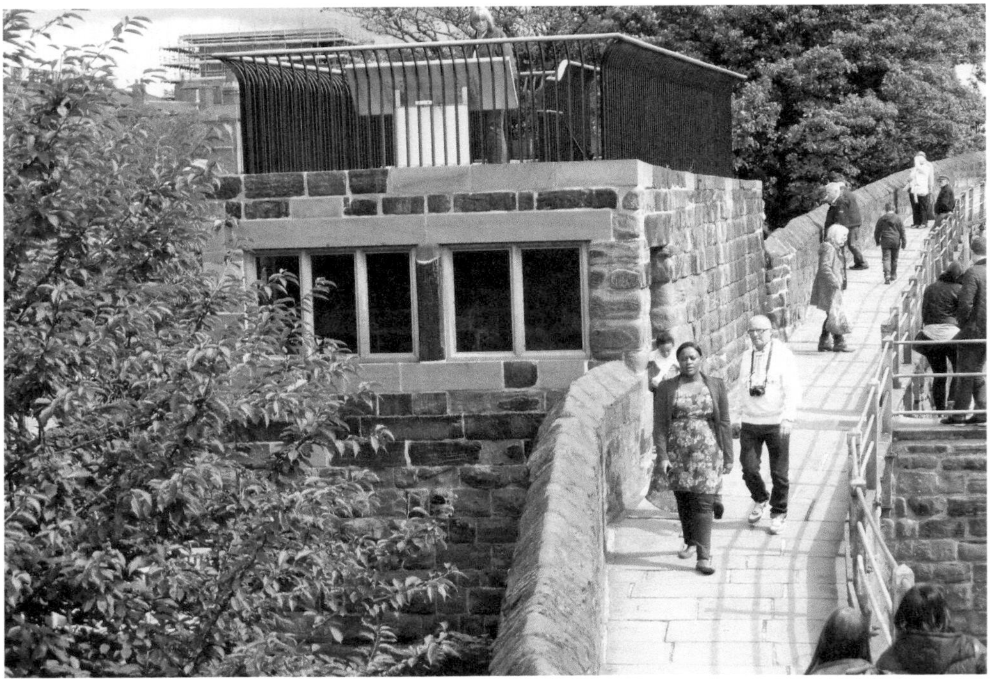

Exterior view of Morgan's Mount gun emplacement, built to defend Royalist Chester. (Courtesy of Dave Craven)

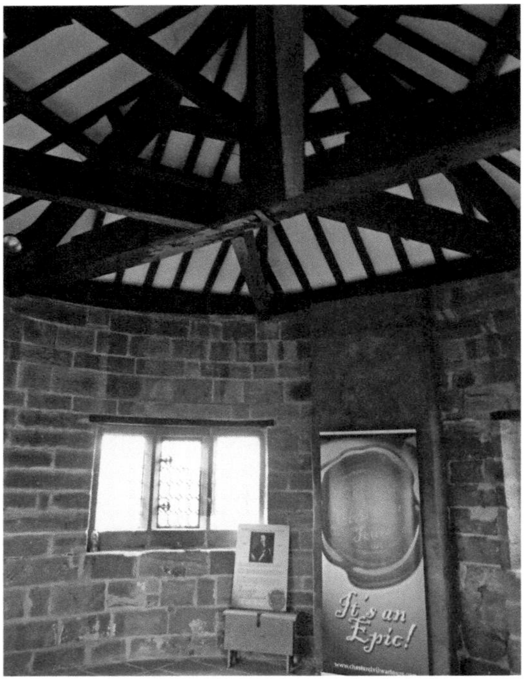

Interior view of Morgan's Mount, on Chester city walls. (Courtesy of Chris McKenna)

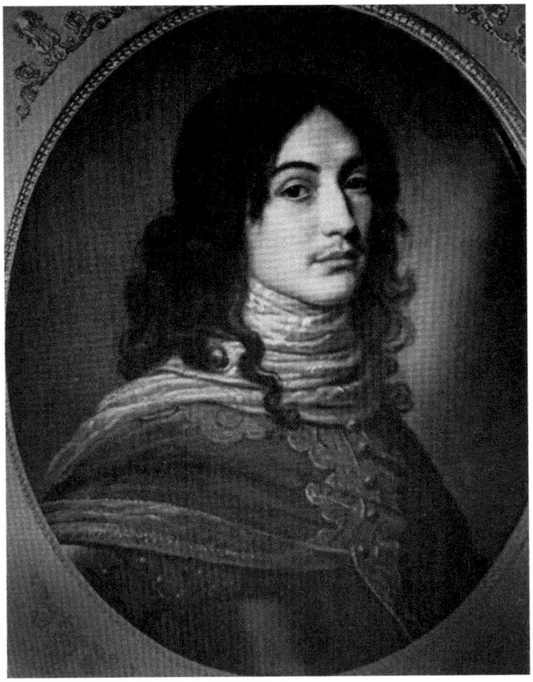

Prince Maurice of Nassau, by unknown artist.

taking many of Byron's best soldiers with him. The royal garrison left behind was again attacked by Jones' men on 20 September 1645, when 1,400 Parliamentary dragoons and infantry successfully breached the outer defences of the Eastgate area and began to bombard the city's inner walls. At this point it seemed that Chester was on the verge of surrender, but on 23 September Charles I himself appeared at the head of a 4,000-strong army to relieve the city.

Charles' appearance in Chester was the prelude to the last great battle to take place within sight of the city walls – the Battle of Rowton Heath, fought on 24 September 1645. This particular military engagement was, in reality, a day-long running battle fought at three distinct locations just outside Chester. At dawn on the 24th, the Royalist commander, Sir Marmaduke Langdale, moved south of Chester's city walls with around 3,000 of Charles' men in order to outflank Parliamentary forces besieging eastern Chester. In response to this move, Parliamentary cavalry under Sydenham Poyntz moved up from Shropshire to intercept Langdale, and sporadic fighting between the two forces ensued at Miller's Heath. Meanwhile, Charles had sent reinforcements from Chester to join Langdale, but these forces were also intercepted by Parliamentary troops under the command of Colonel Lothian. This led to a separate battle taking place near the city walls, between Lothian's men and the Royalist reinforcements intended for Langdale. These reinforcements never reached Langdale. By contrast, the Parliamentarians were able to send reinforcements, led by the ubiquitous Michael Jones, to join Sydenham Poyntz's cavalry, which were lined up facing the Royalists at Rowton Heath, 4 miles south of Chester. The Parliamentary army then attacked and smashed the centre of Langdale's

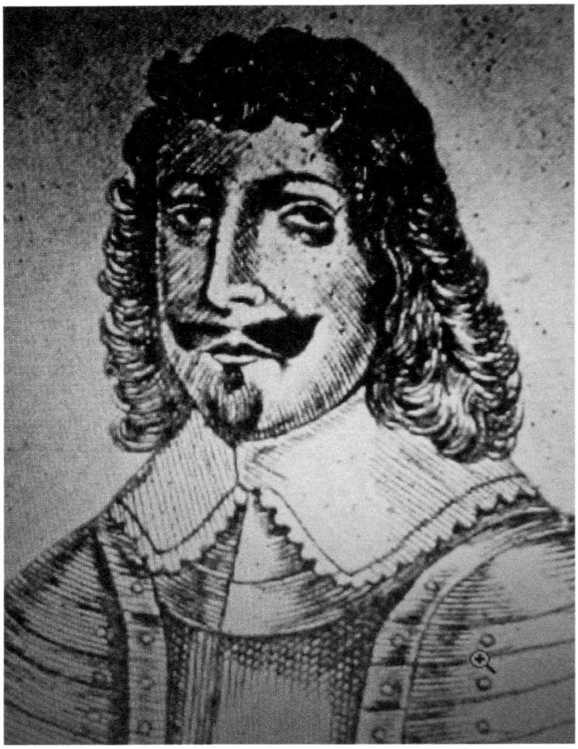

Sydenham Poyntz, from a 1904 illustration by Cornelius Brown.

Royalist army. Some of the Royalists fled into Wales, and others streamed back into Chester. Charles I watched the defeat of his armies from the safety of the Phoenix Tower, on the city walls, and then left Chester with the remainder of his men on 25 September.

Following Charles' defeat at Rowton Heath, the fall of Chester was inevitable, and Parliamentary troops finally entered the city in February 1646. Some looting and killing subsequently took place. Royalist troops were, for example, slaughtered in Ye Olde Boot Inn, on Eastgate Street; but there was no wholesale pillaging of the city, as had happened in Leicester and some other locations across the country. Despite Chester's suffering during the siege of 1645–46, there was still a renewed flowering of Royalist sentiment in 1659, when the city became one of the centres of Sir George Booth's Lancashire- and Cheshire-based revolt against the new English Republic. This revolt was, however, quickly put down by Major-General Lambert, who defeated the rebels at the Battle of Winnington Bridge, near Northwich, in August 1659.

In the period after the end of the English Civil War, military influence in Chester was predictably reduced, despite Jacobite scares in 1715 and 1745. The castle garrison was often very small in size during this period, composed of soldiers with disabilities of one kind or another. As late as 1867, the castle garrison was still a comparatively small one, with probably no more than sixty soldiers from the 54th Foot based within the castle precincts. Nevertheless, by 1810 the Chester Castle area was still transformed as a result of Thomas Harrison's grandiose new neoclassical castle complex, with its armoury

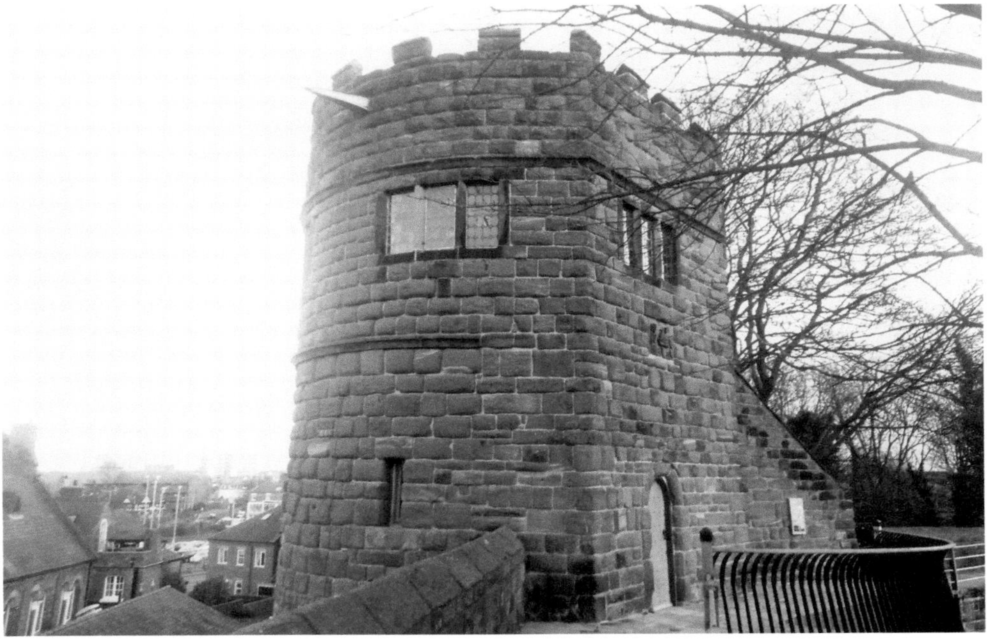

Phoenix/King Charles Tower. (Courtesy of James Merrington)

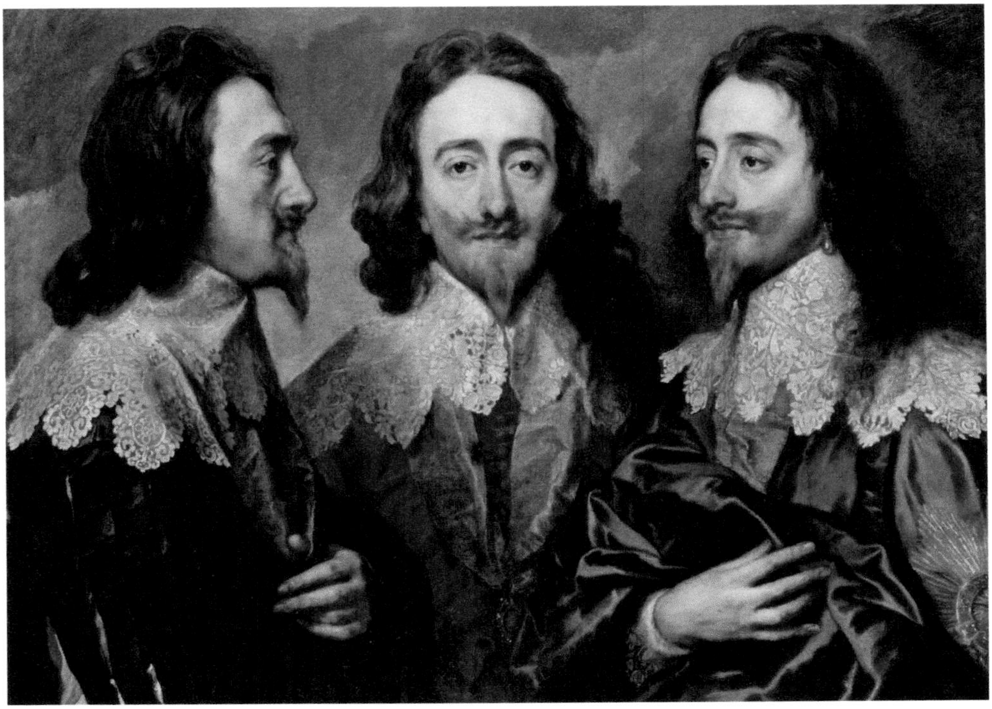

Charles I, by Anthony van Dyck. (© Royal Collection)

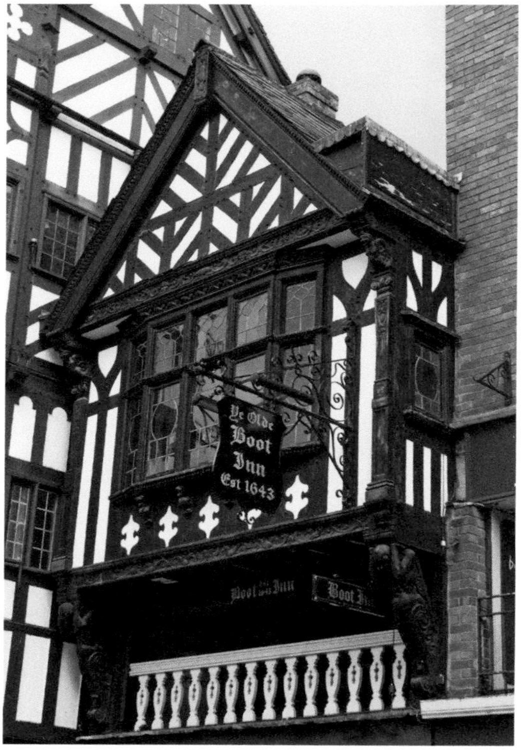

Ye Olde Boot Inn. (Courtesy of Stedent)

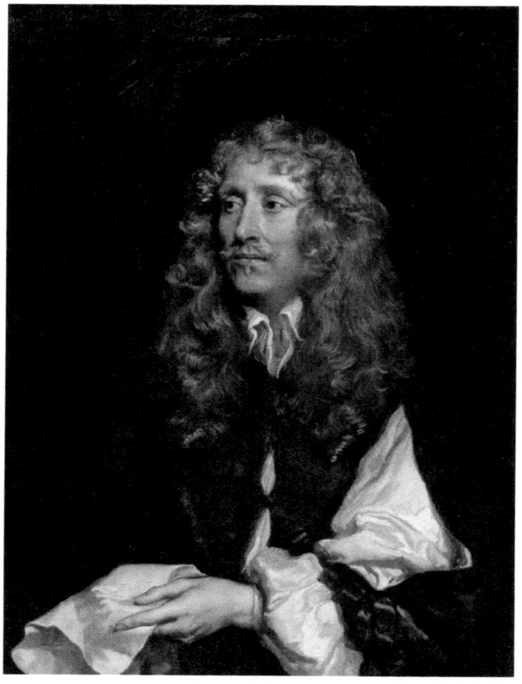

Portrait thought to be of Sir George Booth, by Peter Lely *c.* 1660. (© Art Gallery of South Australia)

and military barracks. The weapons store within the castle armoury was a formidable one, containing as many as 10,000 rifles and 900,000 rounds of ammunition by the mid-nineteenth century. These weapons made a tempting target for the disaffected, and in February 1867 a shadowy and rather mysterious Fenian plot was apparently hatched to seize the weaponry in Chester Castle and then use it to foment insurrection in Ireland.

The Fenian movement, launched in 1858, was a nationalist organisation committed to ending British rule in Ireland, and in early 1867 a Fenian informer told the chief constable of Liverpool, Major Greig, that supporters of the movement were about to seize Chester Castle armoury, on 12 February, and then transport its contents to Ireland via a hijacked train and mail ship. This rather hare-brained scheme was to be launched by between 1,500 and 2,000 Fenian supporters, travelling to Chester by train, in small groups, from Manchester, Liverpool, Crewe and elsewhere. Greig informed the Chester authorities, and the official response was swift and emphatic: the Chester militia and volunteers were mobilised and the castle garrison was reinforced. Seventy regular troops were brought from Manchester, and 500 Scots Guards were raced to Chester from London on a requisitioned train. In addition, 500 special constables were appointed and 150 extra county police were drafted into the city. In the face of this rapid police and military build-up, the Fenians heading to Chester seem simply to have melted away. There were no arrests, and the crisis ended almost before it had begun. This has led some historians to question whether a Fenian 'Chester Plot' actually existed. However, subsequent elements in the Fenians' plans for 1867 did materialise, with small-scale risings taking place in Ireland during March, centred on the town of Tallaght (roughly 12 miles from Dublin). Some newspapers of the time, such as the *Chester Chronicle*, certainly believed in the efficacy of the plot. The British government also rewarded Major Greig for his actions, and the fact that so many troops were rushed to Chester would suggest that both local and

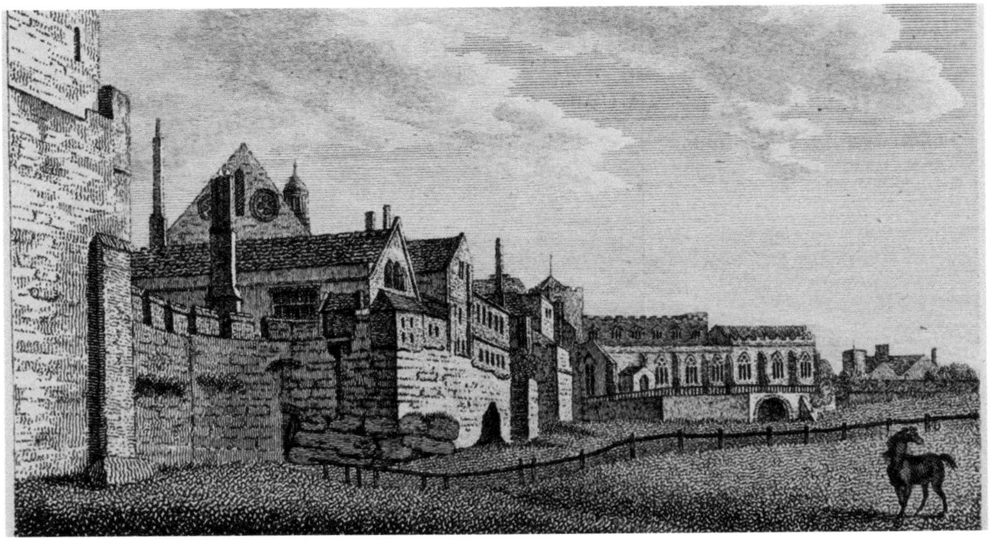

A 1785 view of Chester Castle, before Harrison's reconstruction.

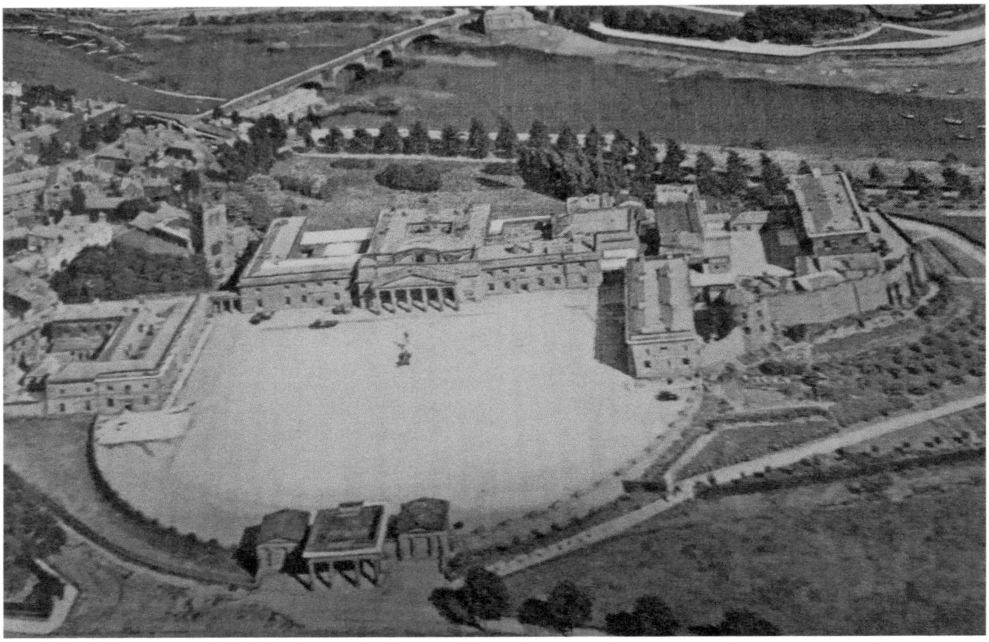

Aerial view of Chester Castle *c.* 1910. (© Cheshire Military Museum)

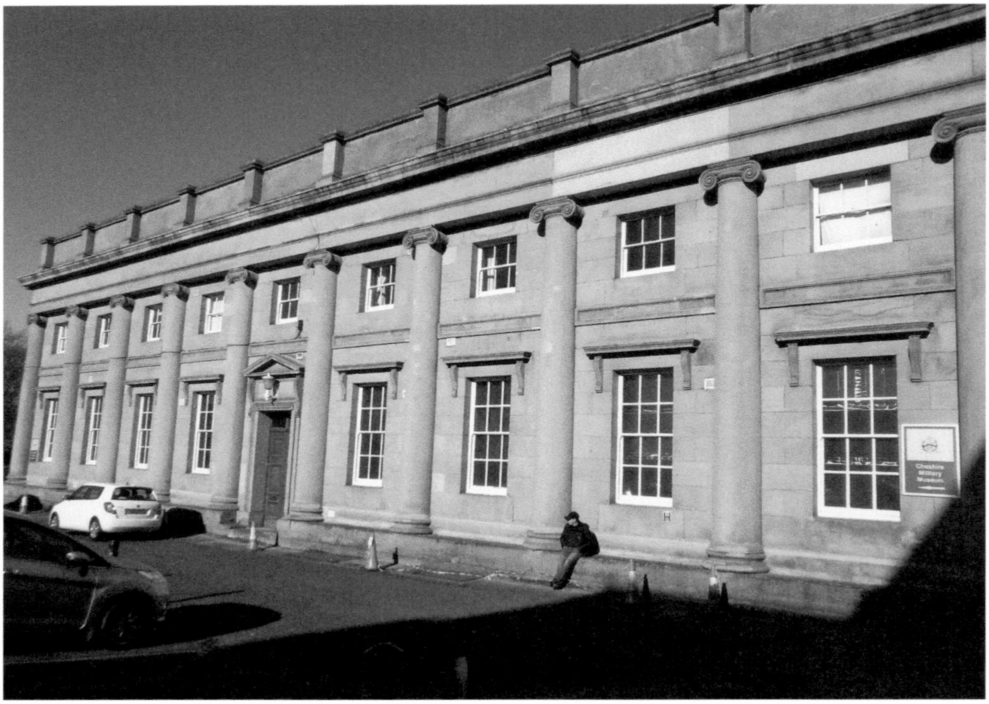

Cheshire Military Museum (formerly Chester Castle barracks).

central government authorities definitely believed that a serious, if somewhat bizarre, Chester-based conspiracy had been thwarted.

The difficulties caused by the ephemeral Fenian Plot of 1867 were as nothing compared to the challenges posed to the city of Chester by the outbreak of the First World War in 1914. No Gotha bombers or Zeppelin airships strafed the city, but in many respects Chester was still in the front line of the war against the Kaiser's Germany. Once Britain had declared war against Germany, in August 1914, hundreds of men flocked into Chester to join the army. The gates of Chester Castle were thronged with men awaiting the issue of their army kit, and large crowds lined the city walls in order to watch military exercises taking place on the Roodee. Once these initial volunteers had marched away to war, Chester Castle remained as the garrison home of the Cheshire Regiment (the regimental garrison remained at the castle until its departure to Dale Road Barracks in 1939). In addition, the city also housed army top brass at Western Command, an army headquarters based at Watergate House, until 1938, which exercised military control over a huge area of western Britain – from Cumberland in the north to Gloucestershire in the south-west.

Like many other British cities, Chester recruited significant numbers of men to fight in the various military and naval campaigns of the war. The city then went on to play a notable role in dealing with the massive casualties of these campaigns: a specific platform at Chester railway station, located behind the Queens Hotel, was allocated for the reception of large numbers of wounded armed forces personnel. These wounded and broken men were then transferred to a range of local buildings – from mansions to workhouses – which had been specially converted into wartime hospitals. In the first

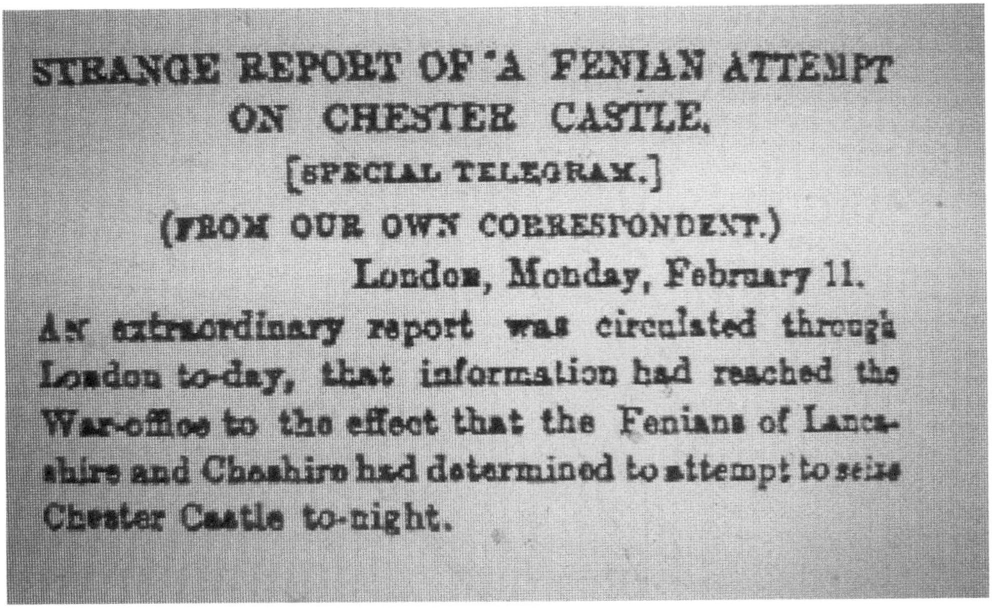

STRANGE REPORT OF A FENIAN ATTEMPT ON CHESTER CASTLE.

[SPECIAL TELEGRAM.]

(FROM OUR OWN CORRESPONDENT.)

London, Monday, February 11.

An extraordinary report was circulated through London to-day, that information had reached the War-office to the effect that the Fenians of Lancashire and Cheshire had determined to attempt to seize Chester Castle to-night.

Contemporary London newspaper report of the 1867 Fenian Plot.

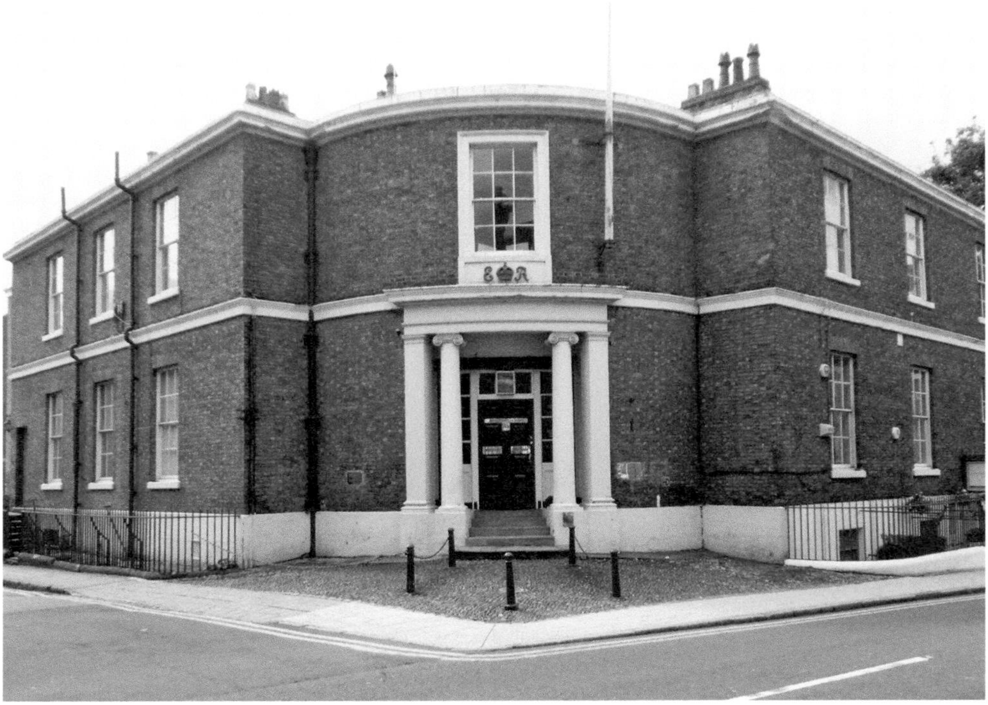

Watergate House, Western Command. (Courtesy of Dave Craven)

year of the war, Hoole Bank House was converted by its owner, George Hayes (at his own expense), in order to cater for the wartime wounded. Other former 'high end' homes of the rich and affluent, such as Eaton Hall, Oakfield House, Carden Park and Saighton Grange were also used to accommodate the spiralling numbers of wounded. At the other end of the architectural spectrum, in 1917 the Chester Union Workhouse was transformed into the Chester War Hospital, with 550 beds to accommodate military casualties. By 1918, 190 staff, drawn from the workhouse, Red Cross, and the Royal Army Medical Corps, were all working at the institution, which had treated over 1,000 patients by May 1919. In addition to coping with the influx of thousands of wounded armed forces personnel, Chester also catered for those psychologically scarred by the ravages of industrialised warfare. What was formerly called the Chester Lunatic Asylum (now part of the Countess of Chester's Hospital) was used to accommodate some of those tragic individuals whose minds and sanity had been unhinged by the effects of shellshock and other psychological traumas.

Not only British troops – able-bodied and wounded – were present in the Chester area, however. During the First World War (as in the Second) Chester catered for a small number of enemy prisoners of war. Some 300 captured German military personnel were held at the disused engineering and boiler-making factory once occupied by Willans & Robinson Ltd at Sandycroft, near Chester. This makeshift POW camp lasted for one year, between 1914 and 1915, before the premises were given over to the production of munitions.

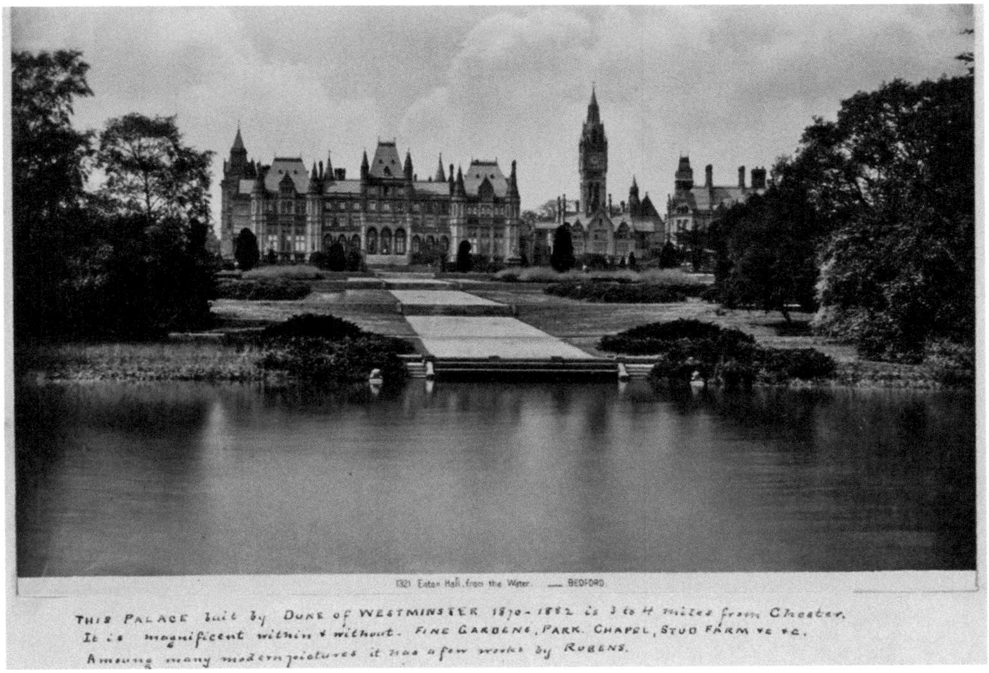

An 1891 photograph of Eaton Hall.

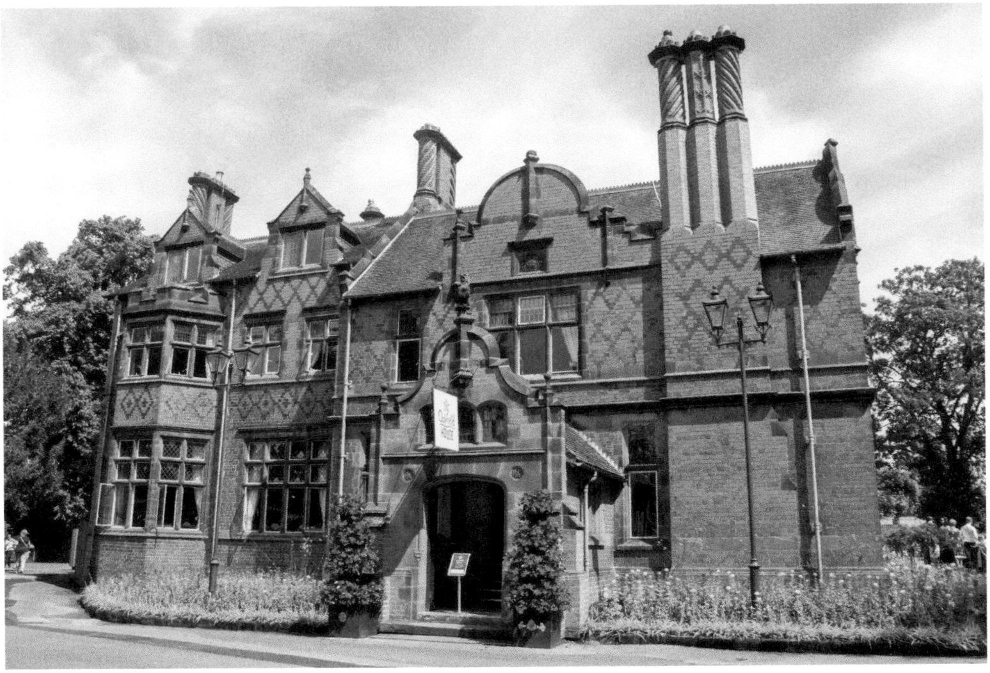

Oakfield Manor. (Courtesy of Mike Peel)

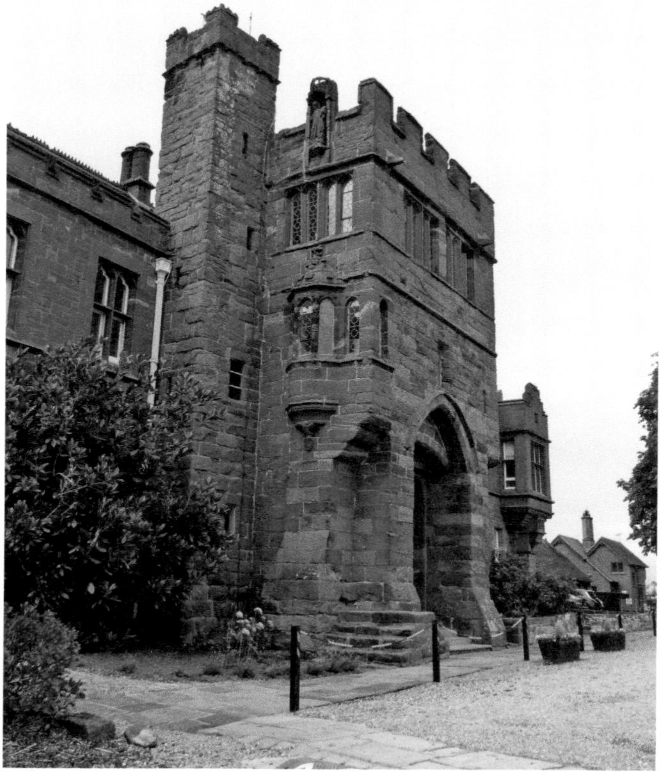

Saighton Grange. (Courtesy of Dave Dunford)

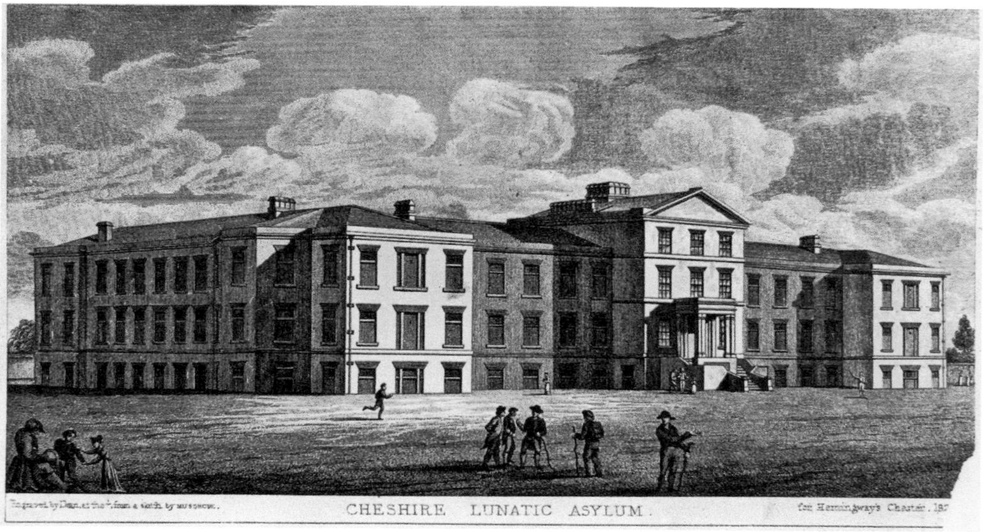

Chester Lunatic Asylum, operational between 1829 and 1921. (© Welcome Library, London)

The Second World War presented even more challenges for the city of Chester than did the 1914–18 war. For a start, the city was actually bombed. Between 1939 and 1945, a total of 232 air-raid alerts were recorded in Chester, and forty-four high-explosive bombs and three incendiaries were dropped on the city. In the two most serious raids of 1940 and 1941, six people were killed and a further six were seriously injured. Such casualty figures were certainly light when compared to the death and destruction inflicted on some other historic British cities. The comparative paucity of the German aerial assault on Chester is perhaps surprising given the fact that there were a number of key RAF stations dotted around the peripheries of the city. There were, for example, 2,578 air force personnel based at RAF Sealand, near Queensferry, in 1940. Flying Training Schools, two Maintenance Units, Searchlight and Anti-Aircraft training facilities were present at the site, which became one of the busiest RAF stations in the whole country. Over 1,000 personnel were also based at RAF Poulton, which was situated on the Duke of Westminster's Eaton Hall estate, and No. 7 Operational Training Unit was located at RAF Hawarden, in Flintshire. All these RAF stations existed in close proximity to the major Vickers-Armstrong aircraft factory at Broughton, near Chester, which produced 5,786 Wellington bombers during the course of the war. These thousands of RAF personnel, male and female, who flocked into Chester on leave days, certainly contributed to the rich martial heritage of the area.

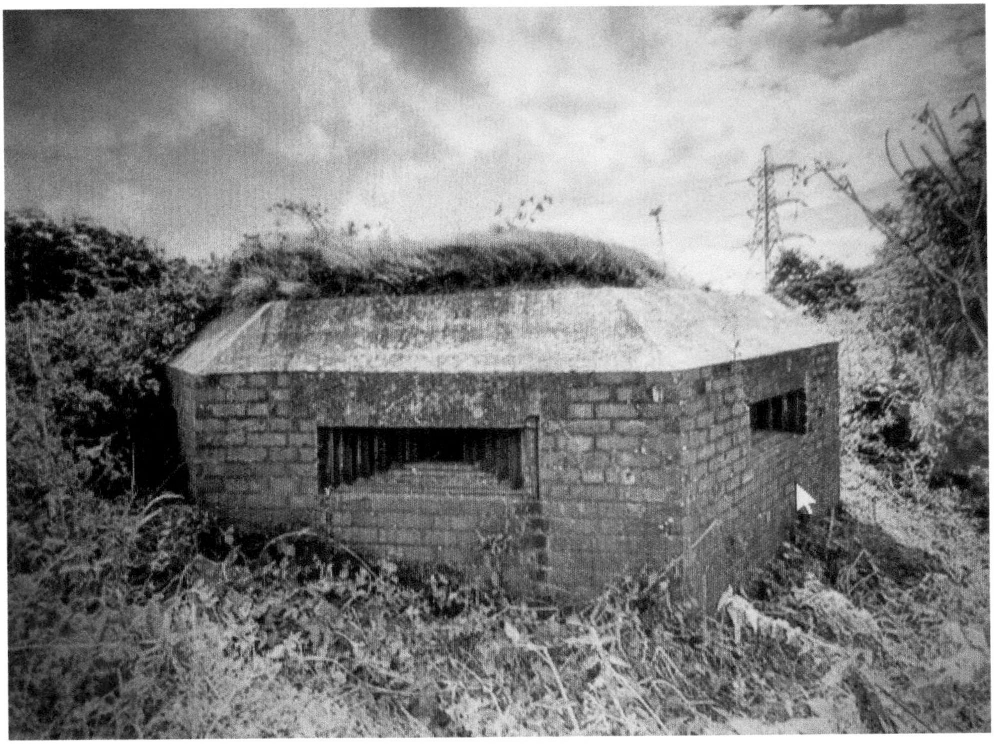

RAF Sealand Second World War pillbox defences. (Courtesy of Mike Searle)

The multinational nature of the armed forces present in Chester was also added to by the many soldiers, sailors and airmen who arrived in the area from the German-occupied countries of Europe. Czech forces were based in and around Cholmondeley Castle, and a memorial to their wartime endeavours was unveiled at Chester Cathedral in 1980. Considerable numbers of Polish pilots and aircrew were also stationed at RAF Sealand (476 by the end of 1943) and Poles, Czechs, Free French, Canadians and other Commonwealth nationalities were trained at nearby RAF Hawarden's No. 7 Training Unit. Chester's wartime military mix was enriched even further by the arrival of American forces in the area during 1942. The main American base was established at camps in and around Hoole Bank House, and significant other US forces were stationed at Vicars Cross. Of course, British armed forces continued to be stationed in and around Chester, and the Western Command building (on Queensway from 1938 onwards), with its impressive array of subterranean bunkers, became an even more important administrative and planning hub for the British army. Naval cadets and staff from the Britannia Royal Navy College were also in Chester, between 1943 and 1946, having been rehoused at Eaton Hall following bomb damage to the college's premises in Dartmouth, Devon. Certainly, by the end of the Second World War the overall military presence in Chester was more multinational, and multi-ethnic, than at any time since the Romans had first established their settlement at Deva in the first century CE.

6. Queens, Marines, Warlords and Weapons

For well over a thousand years, men and women from a range of backgrounds have contributed massively to the rich martial heritage of the city of Chester. Some of these people were born in Chester, others were not. Regardless of their birthplace, however, all the people mentioned below had a significant impact upon matters of either military, naval or aerial warfare, which extended far beyond the city of Chester itself.

Queen Aethelflaed of the Mercians

Aethelflaed was the eldest daughter of Alfred the Great, king of Wessex between CE 878 and 899. She had four siblings, and proved to be a clever, resourceful girl from an early age. Aethelflaed was given a good education at Alfred's Court, despite being female (which was unusual for the time). She was probably born in CE 870 and was married to King Aethelred of Mercia when she was around fifteen or sixteen years old. England in the ninth century was a divided land, split between rival Saxon kingdoms, and with the invading Viking settlers ensconced in the lands beyond the Danelaw. The kingdom of Mercia lay to the north of Alfred's Wessex and contained lands in the Midlands, north-west and south-east, with Chester at the north-west extremity of its domains and London – wrested from the Danes by Alfred in CE 889 and given to Mercia – at its south-eastern tip.

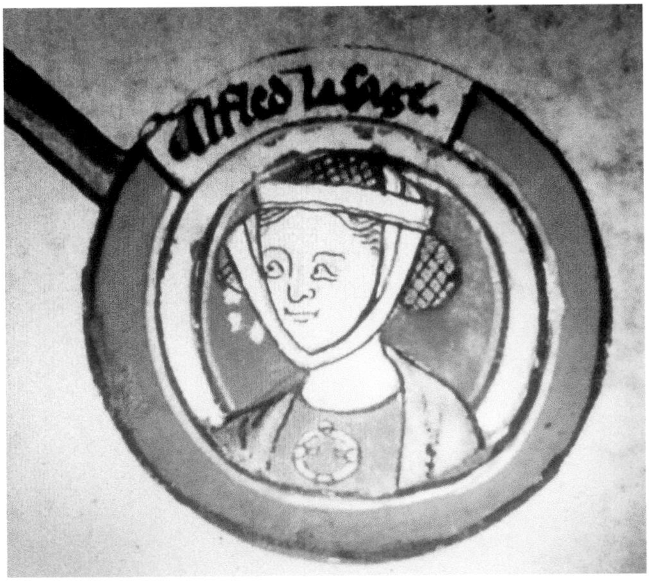

Medieval miniature of Aethelflaed.

Aethelflaed was every inch the warrior queen. She went with her armies on campaign and was the de facto ruler of Mercia from CE 902 onwards, when her husband Aethelred was permanently incapacitated by illness. Aethelflaed worked with her husband prior to his illness to push back the Danes and later in her military career she worked with her brother Edward, when he was king of Wessex, to achieve the same goals.

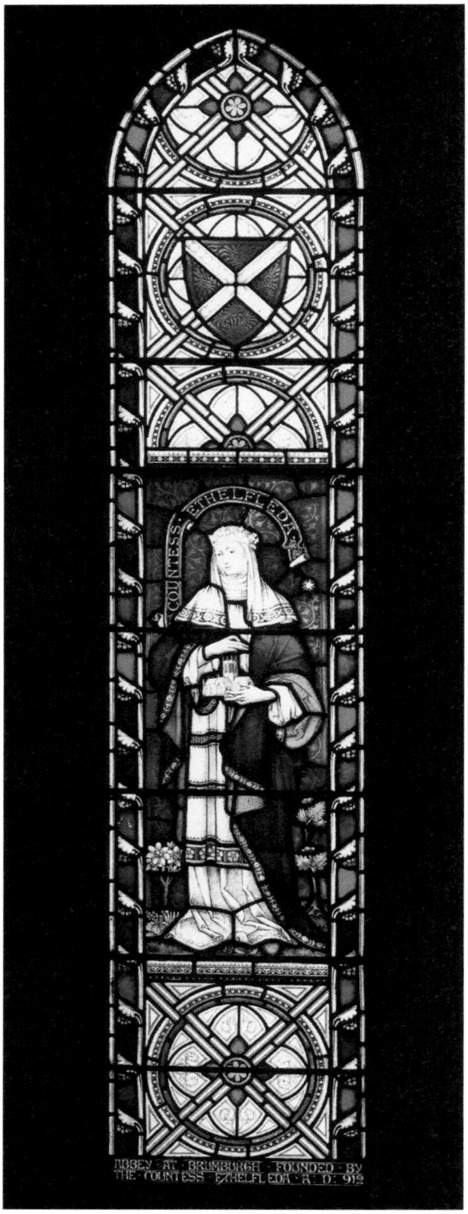

Stained-glass depiction of Aethelflaed, St Barnabas Church, Bromborough. (Courtesy of Dave Craven)

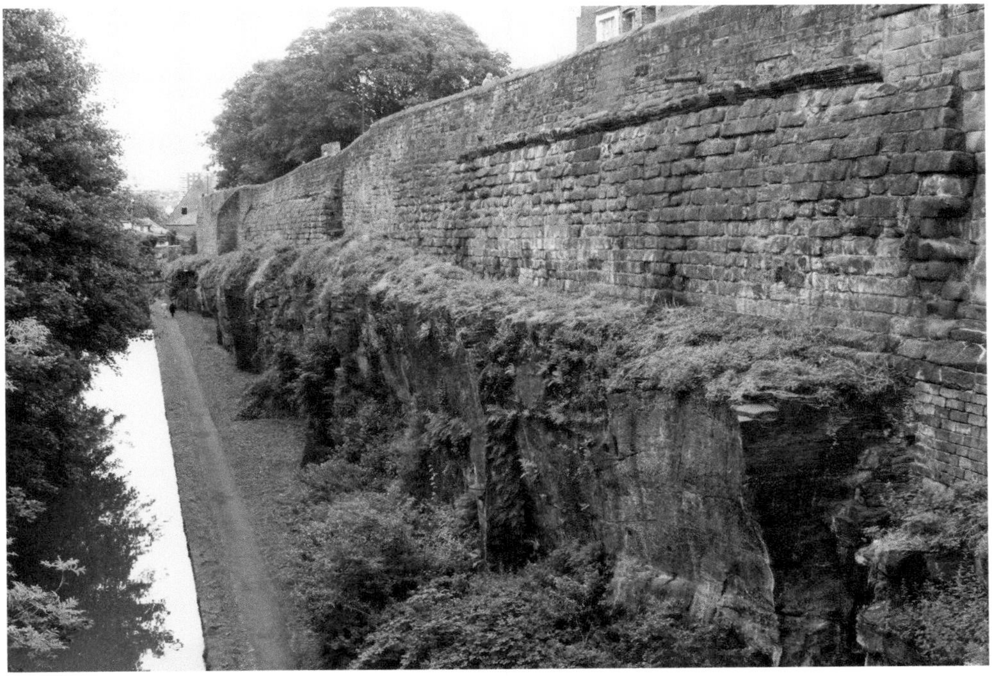

Chester city walls, from Northgate to the Phoenix Tower. (Courtesy of Wolfgang Sauber)

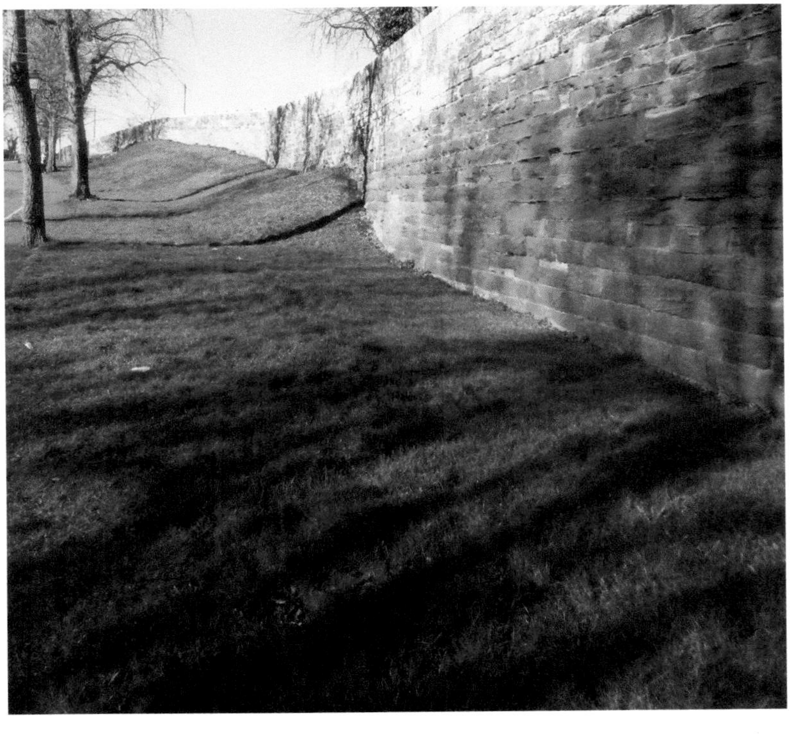

City walls near the castle.

Her response to a crisis in Chester, in CE 907, proved to have some momentous strategic and military consequences. At some point prior to CE 907 Aethelflaed had allowed groups of Vikings from Dublin, led by Ingimund, to settle on the Wirral Peninsula, possibly in an effort to win their loyalty in any future struggle with the Danes. These new settlers could also be used as a buffer to prevent further Danish incursions into Mercian territory in the north-west, via the River Mersey. During CE 907, this policy backfired badly, as Ingimund and his Viking army attempted to seize the city of Chester by force. Aethelflaed's response was swift and decisive. A Mercian army was despatched to Chester to defend the city and to defeat the Vikings; however, Aethelflaed's role in the defence of Chester involved much more than merely sending an army. She may well have accompanied her warriors to Chester, as she did to many other locations. In addition, contemporary sources such as the Irish Annals suggest that she was also principally responsible for the military tactics and overall strategy that defeated the Vikings at Chester. Politically, Aethelflaed made some very astute moves, which had the effect of turning the Dublin Vikings against the Vikings camped outside Chester's walls. Militarily, Aethelflaed also carried out an astute strategy of feint and counter feint, which would have been recognised by army generals in both ancient and modern times. The Mercian army fought the Viking force outside Chester's walls, and the gates to the city were intentionally left open. Presumably after some kind of prearranged signal, the Mercians feigned a retreat into the city, and were followed by the undisciplined Vikings. Mercian cavalry had been secretly brought into the city before the battle, and they then emerged to slaughter the trapped Vikings. Aethelflaed's victory was complete. It was also a victory assisted by the inhabitants of Chester, who dropped boiling beer and beehives from the city walls onto the unfortunate Vikings below.

Aethelflaed followed up her crucial strategic victory at Chester by rebuilding the city's walls. This rebuilding represented a continuation of King Alfred's policy of establishing burghs (fortified towns) to support and protect Saxon settlements from encroachment by the Vikings. It proved to be a remarkably successful policy and helped lead to the establishment of a unified Saxon kingdom of England under Aethelstan (who was Aethelflaed's nephew) in CE 924. The successful defence of Chester in CE 907 was one of her finest achievements. Over 1,000 years later, in the twenty-first century, the fact that Chester has the UK's only complete perimeter city walls is due in no small part to the inspiration provided by Aethelflaed, the so-called 'lady of the Mercians'.

Hugh d'Avranches, Earl of Chester

Hugh d'Avranches, sometimes known as Hugh Lupus (the Wolf) because of his savagery in battle against the Welsh, and less flatteringly as Hugh le Gros (the Fat) because of his propensity to gluttony, was born in the mid-1040s in Avranches, Normandy. He was the son of Richard le Goz, Count of Avranches, a prominent Norman aristocrat who funded between thirty and sixty of the ships William the Conqueror used to invade England in 1066. By the 1060s, Hugh was already a close confidante of William the Conqueror. He stayed loyal to the Crown during the great rebellion of 1088, and he also proved to be a steadfast and loyal councillor to the Conqueror's successors, William Rufus and Henry I.

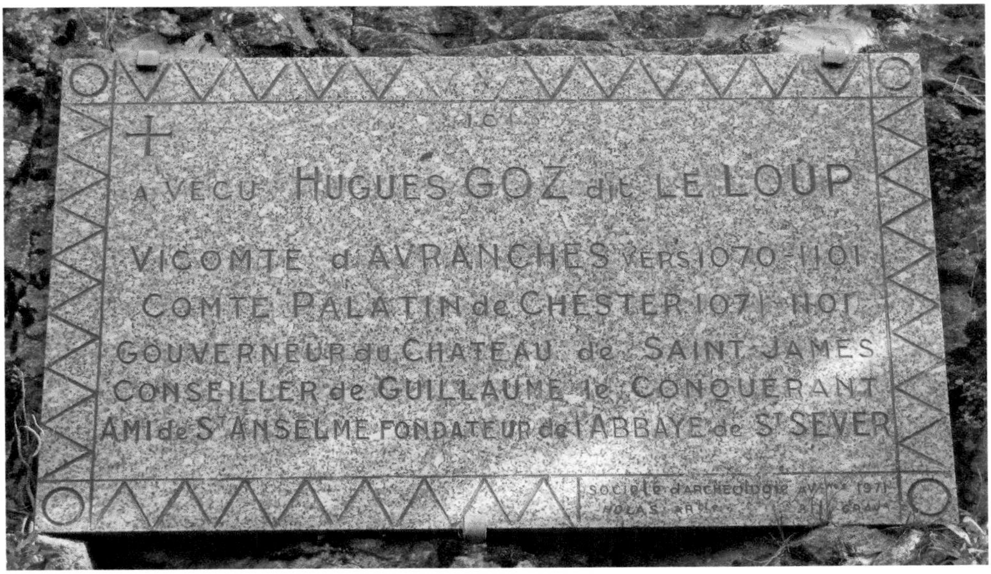

Hugh Lupus plaque, Avranches, Normandy.

In 1071, William the Conqueror gave Hugh the earldom of Chester, which was a key position in early Norman England. The settlement of Chester was strategically placed on the Marcher borders with Wales, and needed a strong hand to rule it. Hugh was given quasi-regal powers to rule in what was known as the County Palatine of Chester. His word was law, and there were very few limitations as to what Hugh could and couldn't do with his powers derived 'of the palace'.

Although Gerbold the Fleming had briefly been Earl of Chester between 1069 and 1071, Hugh d'Avranches was really the first significant Marcher Earl of Chester, occupying the position for thirty years, between 1071 and 1101. Militarily, he set the pattern for future earls (and monarchs such as Edward I) by attempting the subjugation of the nearby Welsh of Gwynedd and north Wales. Hugh was frequently on campaign in Wales, alongside his cousin Robert of Rhuddlen, and Norman forces under their control successfully took over most of northern Wales (at least for a short time). In 1081, they captured Gruffudd ap Cynon, king of Gwynedd, and Hugh imprisoned the unfortunate king in Chester Castle for the next twelve years. Following Gruffudd's capture, it was Robert rather than Hugh who ruled over much of Wales. In 1093, however, Robert of Rhuddlen was killed in a fight with the Welsh, near the Great Orme, on the north Welsh coast. For a short time, Hugh took over Robert's lands. He left behind him his responsibilities in Chester and his vast estates in Cheshire and the Midlands, and moved through Wales with a small but well-equipped army. One contemporary chronicler recalled that at this time 'Hugh took wholeheartedly to his newfound wealth, and indulged himself totally in food, hunting and women'. Hugh didn't live off the fat of the (Welsh) land for long, though. Gruffudd, king of Gwynedd, escaped from Chester Castle in 1094 and was still in strong enough physical shape to lead a Welsh revolt, which recovered all the lands previously lost to Hugh, Earl of Chester, and

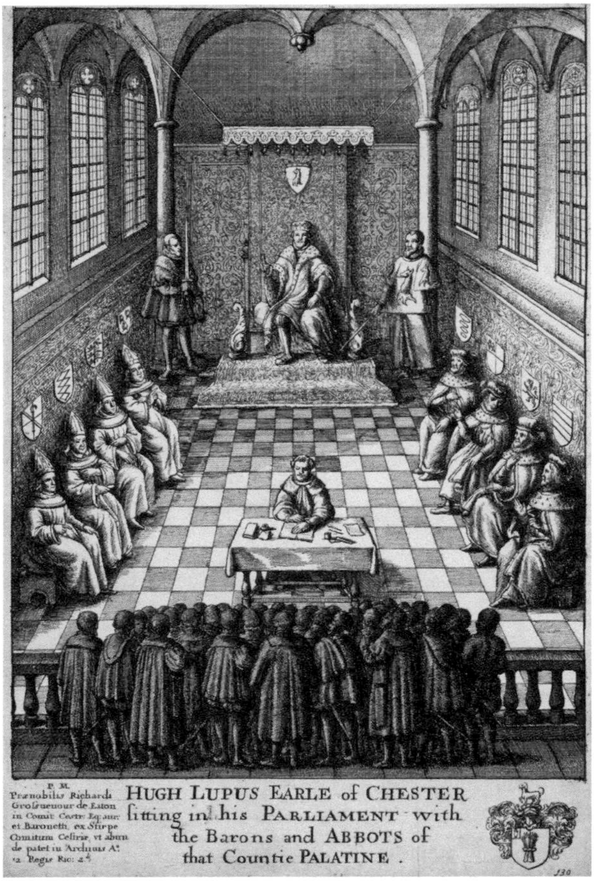

Hugh Lupus, by Wenceslaus Hollar. (© Thomas Fisher Rare Book Library)

Robert of Rhuddlan. Hugh had to wait another five years before he could again exercise his ruthless wolf-like tendencies in battle against the Welsh. In 1098, he left Cheshire to join forces with another Norman warlord, Hugh the Red of Montgomery, the 2nd Earl of Shrewsbury. Their combined forces invaded Gwynedd territory and forced Gruffudd to flee to Ireland. Ultimately, however, this whole Norman campaign ended in failure when Magnus Barefoot, king of Norway, intervened on the side of the Welsh. The Earl of Shrewsbury was killed in battle against Magnus's forces on the eastern side of the Menai Straits, and the Normans were forced to leave Welsh territory. Gruffudd returned as ruler of Gwynedd, and Hugh, Earl of Chester, never attempted to recover the Welsh lands he had formerly occupied.

By the year 1100, the increasingly corpulent Hugh was in no fit state to campaign with his soldiers. He shared many characteristics with his former master, William the Conqueror, who was also aggressive and brutal when he deemed it to be necessary. Both men also had a strong tendency towards corpulence in later life, and both had, rather paradoxically, a strong sense of piety and religiosity. Hugh d'Avranches was a friend of St Anselm, Archbishop of Canterbury between 1093 and 1109. He also endowed monasteries

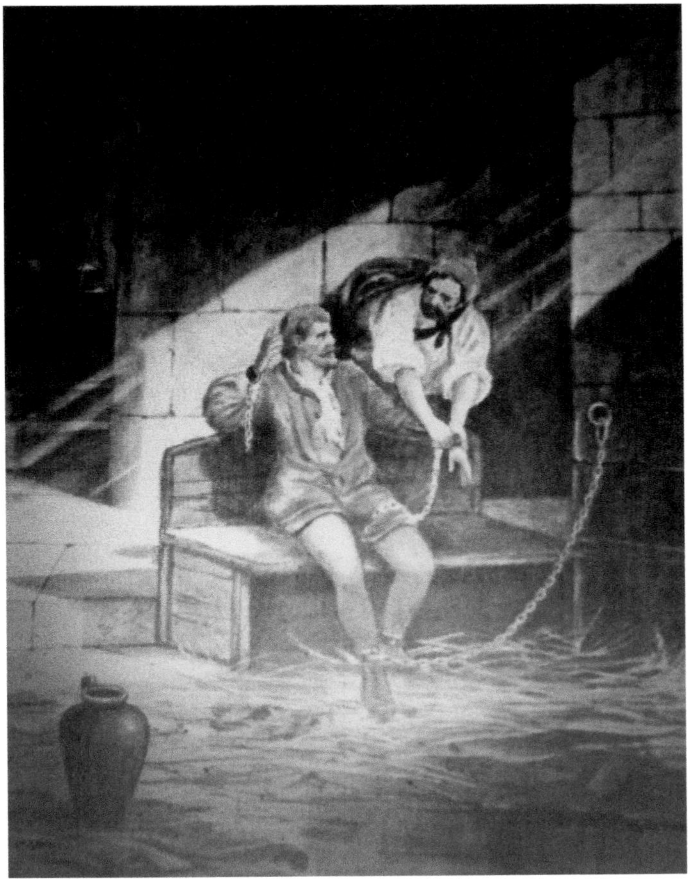

Gruffudd ap Cynan escaping from Chester Castle, by T. Prytherch, 1900.

in Normandy and Yorkshire, and he founded the abbey of St Werburgh in Chester. As Hugh's health began to decline, he decided to give up the trappings of military power in order to become a monk in 1101. Within a few days of assuming this new religious role, Hugh Lupus, Chester's first great Norman warlord, was dead. He was succeeded as Earl of Chester by his son, Richard, who dominated the County Palatine of Chester (and much else besides) until his untimely death in the *White Ship* disaster of 1120.

John and Eleanor Byron

John Byron was born in 1599 to a well-to-do Lancashire gentry family, which later resettled in Nottinghamshire. He served as Nottinghamshire's MP in the Parliaments of 1624 and 1628, and he acted as high sheriff of Nottinghamshire in 1634. By the late 1630s, however, it was John Byron's military career, rather than his political aspirations, which became of paramount importance. During the period of the first English Civil War, between 1642 and 1646, Byron became one of Charles I's most important Royalist generals. In October 1643, he was appointed field marshal of the Royalist armies in Cheshire, Lancashire and north Wales, and between 1644 and 1646 he commanded the Royalist garrison in Chester, which was besieged by Parliamentary forces under Sir William Brereton. Control of the city of Chester was vital for the Royalist cause during the Civil War. It provided a key link to the Royalist heartlands of north Wales, and after the surrender of Bristol to Parliament in September 1645, Chester was the one Royalist port left by which troops could be disembarked from service in Ireland and fed into the struggle against Parliament in England. As such, Charles I needed a seasoned, experienced commander in charge of Chester, and few were more experienced, or had more battlefield experience, than John Byron. The ex-MP had fought for Charles I since the very beginning of the Civil War, when the king had raised his royal standard at Nottingham on 22 August 1642. Indeed, Byron had fought for Charles I before this period, leading a troop of horse against Scottish enemies of the king, during the 1639–40 Bishops' Wars. Once fighting began in England, Byron's skills as a cavalry commander were called upon repeatedly by the king. He fought in many of the war's key engagements, including Edgehill, Roundway Down, the first battle of Newbury, and Marston Moor. Byron was often in the thick of the fighting, and received a savage halberd wound to the left part of his face during a skirmish at Burford in Oxfordshire, in January 1643. As a reward for his exemplary military service, Charles I made John Byron the 1st Baron Byron of Rochdale later in the same year. The man given charge of the royal bastion of Chester was clearly a talented and brave commander.

Until Charles I's army was defeated at Rowton Heath in September 1645 Byron had managed to keep the River Dee bridge route to Wales open. As a result, Chester had not

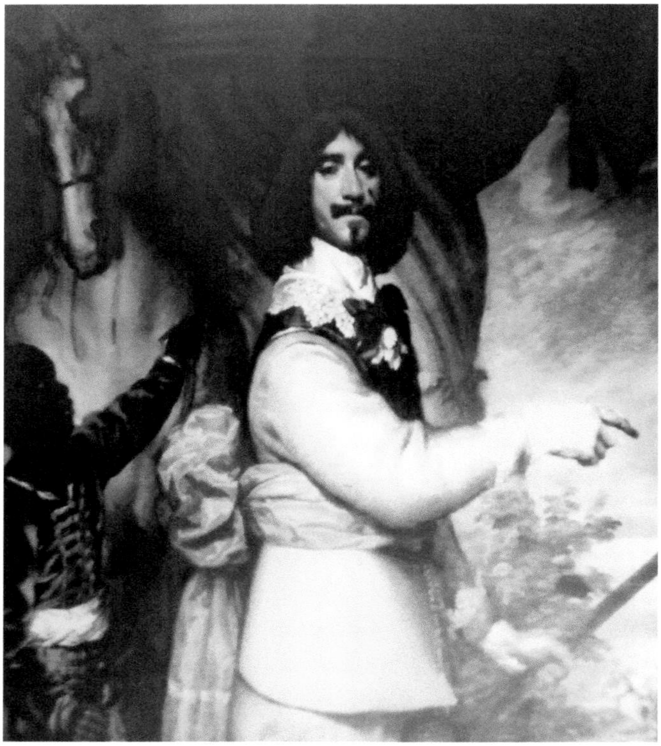

John Byron, from a contemporary portrait.

been fully encircled and besieged. After Rowton Heath, though, the net was tightened, and Chester was surrounded entirely by Parliamentary forces. Even then, when the situation seemed entirely hopeless, Byron refused to give up. He maintained a spirited, strategically skilful defence of the city, despite overwhelming odds, throughout the autumn and winter of 1645. There were repeated Royalist sallies out of the city, to destroy Parliamentarian siege works and gun emplacements. Even so, Chester was still being bombarded night and day, and troops and civilians were dying of starvation and disease. A more enlightened and compassionate commander might well have surrendered Chester in order to spare the populace from unnecessary suffering. Byron, however, had a reputation for ruthlessness and brutality. He was known as the 'Bloody Braggadocio' after apparently boasting about the slaughter of Parliamentary supporters at Barthomley Church following the 1643 Battle of Middlewich. Byron seemed unconcerned about the plight of Chester's civilians, and in return, the non-combatants of the city seemed to have heartedly disliked Baron Byron. It took all the Chester mayor's persuasive skills to force Byron to yield to the inevitable and surrender the city to Parliament in January 1646.

Following the surrender, John Byron fled through north Wales to Anglesey. On Anglesey, he tried to set up another tough and uncompromising Royalist regime, replicating his style of control in Chester. This aroused the hostility of the Anglesey population, and there was at least one plot to assassinate Byron during his time on the island. The former Chester garrison commander finally left Wales for exile in France in June 1646. He never returned to Britain and died unexpectedly in Paris (of unknown causes) in 1652.

In 1644, John Byron had taken time away from his military duties in order to marry Eleanor Needham, the seventeen-year-old widow of Peter Warburton, a prominent member of the Cheshire gentry. Subsequently, Eleanor joined John at Chester and shared with him the privations of the siege of the city. Indeed, Eleanor played a distinguished role in trying to help her battle-hardened husband during the siege. In December 1645, at the height of the siege, when Chester was entirely blockaded by Parliamentary forces, Eleanor slipped out of the city in disguise, moved through the Parliamentary lines, and travelled 151 miles to Oxford to seek help from the king. At this late stage in the war, Charles could do little to help, so Eleanor's efforts were in vain. Nevertheless, it was still an epic journey for a teenage girl to make in wartime. Eleanor Byron showed the same spirit and determination once the fighting was over, and she had joined her husband in exile in Paris. Although she remained loyal to her husband during his lifetime, she later became one of Charles Stuart's many mistresses, in the period before he returned to England as King Charles II in 1660. Once the future king had tired of her, Eleanor refused to go quietly and demanded £15,000 in money and jewels by way of compensation. How much of this astronomical sum Charles II actually managed to pay is uncertain.

Watkin Tench

Watkin Tench was born in Chester in 1758 and was the son of Fisher Tench, a prominent Cestrian who ran a local school and was also a skilled dancing master. The family had some notable military links: Watkin's mother was a member of the Tarleton family from Liverpool, and his cousin was none other than Banastre Tarleton, the operational leader of the British Legion of American loyalists during the American War of Independence (and the man portrayed in a thoroughly inaccurate fashion in Mel Gibson's 1995 Hollywood epic *The Patriot*).

In 1776, young Watkin joined His Majesty's Marines at Plymouth, as a second lieutenant, and embarked upon a naval career every inch as colourful as that followed by the fictional hero Hornblower in the well-known sea-based novels of C. S. Forester. Within two years of joining the marines, Tench had been promoted to first lieutenant and was part of the marine detachment aboard HMS *Mermaid*. During 1778, *Mermaid* was stationed off the eastern seaboard of America and fighting both the Americans (who were struggling to free themselves from British colonial rule) and the French, who had joined the struggle on the side of the Americans. Tench and the *Mermaid* became involved in a sea battle with French forces under Jean Baptiste Hector, comte d'Estaing. The struggle didn't go well for the British, and the *Mermaid* was driven onto the shores of Maryland, where Tench and some of the crew members were captured by the American rebels. Watkin was then taken to Philadelphia, where he was incarcerated for a short time as a prisoner of war, before being returned into British hands as part of a prisoner exchange in October 1778.

The ever-resourceful Tench was immediately back on the high seas, serving on HMS *Unicorn* between October 1778 and March 1779, and in September 1782 he was

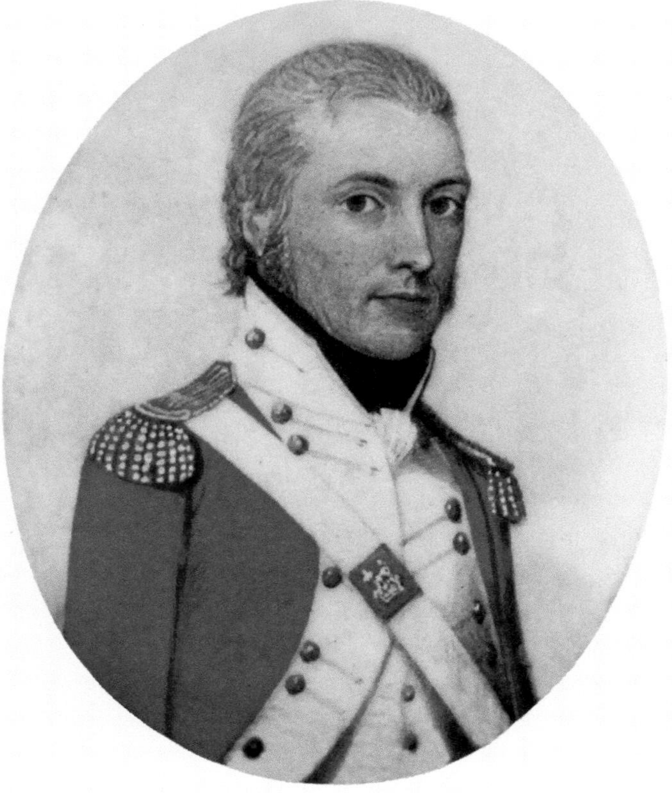

Watkin Tench, *c.* 1800. (© Mitchell State Library, New South Wales)

promoted to the rank of captain-lieutenant. Once the American war ended, however, opportunities for talented marines and naval officers were reduced, and the Chester man was placed on half-pay in May 1786. Faced with the prospect of an impecunious future on half-pay, Watkin Tench took the career defining opportunity of volunteering for a three-year Royal Navy led mission to establish a convict settlement at Botany Bay in Australia. Tench volunteered to join the marine detachment part of this expedition at the end of 1786, and in May 1787 he set sail for Botany Bay as a marine officer on board the transport ship *Charlotte*. Tench and the *Charlotte* were part of Commodore Arthur Philip's famous First Fleet, which landed in Botany Bay in January 1788, to create the first sustainable European settlement in Australia. During his time in Australia, Watkin proved to be much more than just a soldier-sailor. He explored the outback and became the first European to track the course of the Nepean River. In addition, Tench also became an early travel writer of distinction. Before he'd even set sail from England, he secured a deal with Debrett's, the publishers, to write an account of his experiences in Australia. Two highly successful books followed about his adventures in Botany Bay and Port Jackson in New South Wales, which went into multiple editions and were translated into French, German and Dutch.

Tench returned from Australia to England in 1792 and was soon promoted to the rank of brevet-major in the marines. By late 1794, the new brevet-major was back in action, fighting the seaborne forces of Revolutionary France. During November of that year, Tench was acting as a marine officer aboard HMS *Alexander* when it was involved in a desperate sea battle with three French warships. The *Alexander* was defeated by these much superior forces, and Tench (along with his Admiral, Rodney Bligh) was captured and spent the following six months as a prisoner of the French. During this period of captivity Tench again exercised his literary skills and wrote a series of letters from France,

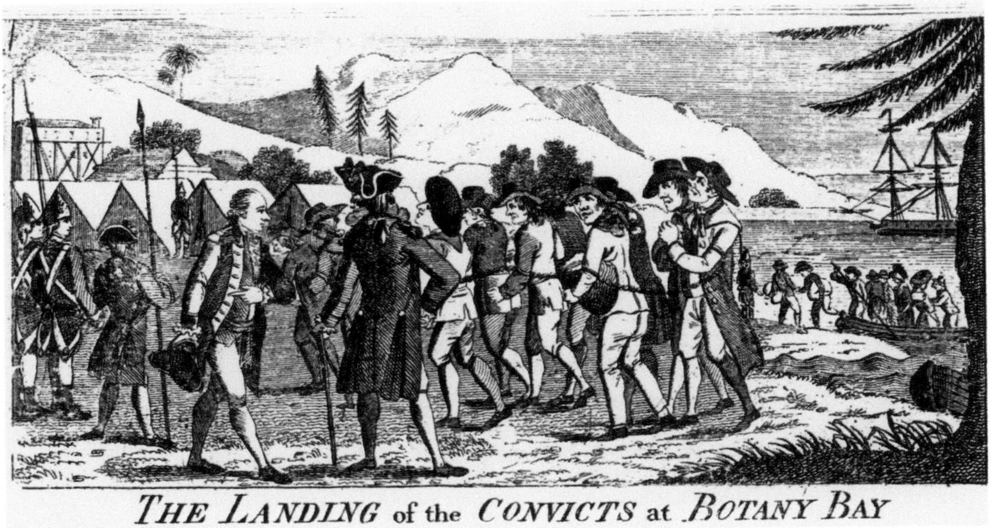

From Watkin Tench's *A Narrative of the Expedition to Botany Bay* (1789).

which were later published under the title *Letters Written in France to a Friend in London*. Watkin was released by the French as part of a prisoner exchange scheme and spent the next four years as a marine officer on board HMS *Polyphemus*, which was engaged on Atlantic and English Channel convoy duties. In 1801, Tench rejoined the fleet blockading the French Channel ports aboard HMS *Princess Royal*, and his career afloat ended the following year when he accepted the first of a series of shore posts at Chatham dockyards.

Further shore postings took Tench to Plymouth and then to Woolwich before he retired with the rank of major-general in late 1815. However, the Royal Navy still wasn't finished with Watkin Tench. In 1819, at the age of sixty-one, he was reactivated as commandant of Plymouth Division, and he continued to serve the navy in a shore-based capacity until 1827, when he finally retired for good with the rank of lieutenant-general. Tench died in Devonport, Plymouth, in 1833, and was without doubt one of the most remarkable martial figures ever to come from Chester. He fought both the French and the Americans with some distinction. In addition, he was a skilled linguist, a keen explorer and a talented writer. Tench and his wife had no children of their own; however, after a lifetime of battling on the high seas, exploration and writing, he became (in late middle age) the adoptive father of four very young children, orphaned by the death of his sister-in-law. The elderly Mr and Mrs Tench seem to have approached the task of looking after these children with considerable care, love and attention.

John Dolphin

The role of technical experts such as engineers, scientists and mathematicians in modern warfare, is often indispensable. John Robert Vernon Dolphin, born in 1905 in the small village of Christleton, just outside Chester, was just such a technical expert. He was born into a well-to-do scientific family, with a father who worked as a metallurgist for a copper refining company. John grew up to be an inventor and engineer of some brilliance. After leaving school, he enrolled as a student apprentice at Loughborough Engineering College, where he successfully graduated at the age of twenty-one. Two years of employment followed at the Hydraulic Engineering Company in Chester, and Dolphin then occupied a series of progressively more responsible positions in the engineering sector until he became a self-employed consultant in 1938. John Dolphin's successful civilian career in engineering was combined with a burgeoning military career in the Territorial Army (TA). In 1928, he was commissioned as a second lieutenant in the 4/5th TA Battalion of the Cheshire Regiment, and in 1931 he was promoted to lieutenant in the same regiment. Once war broke out in September 1939 Dolphin received a series of temporary wartime promotions, becoming a captain and then a major, and in July 1942 he was promoted to the rank of lieutenant-colonel. John Dolphin's meteoric rise in the army owed much to his engineering prowess, but also acted as a cover for his significant role within the shadowy world of the Special Operations Executive (SOE). The SOE was a clandestine organisation set up by Winston Churchill in 1940 with the declared aim of 'setting German occupied Europe ablaze'. Dolphin became a key member of this secret organisation. By the end of 1939 he was living at No. 97, The Frythe, near Welwyn in Hertfordshire, and was described in military documentation of the time as being a civil servant, working for the War Office.

In fact, The Frythe (an exclusive former hotel) had been requisitioned by the British government and become the wartime home of SOE's Station IX, which was responsible for secret weapons development. John Dolphin was engaged in all sorts of secret research on military vehicles, equipment, explosives and sabotage, and during 1943 he became the commanding officer at the station. All the often-deadly items produced at Station IX by Dolphin and his associates were given names prefixed by 'Wel' in order to show The Frythe's proximity to the nearby town of Welwyn.

Some of the weapons developed under Dolphin at Station IX were undoubtedly very successful; for example, the Welrod was the particular brainchild of Major Hugh Reeves, and proved to be a simple, reliable and quiet gun, ideal for assassination purposes. There were no markings on the Welrod, which was used extensively by the SOE, the American OSS (forerunners of the CIA) and by European Resistance forces. There were 2,800 Welrods made during the Second World War, and another 14,000 were produced in the post-war period. Dolphin was a keen motorcyclist, and closely involved in the development of the Welbike, a small folding motorcycle that could be dropped from the air in containers and then unpacked and used by paratroopers. Dolphin's Welbike was the smallest motorcycle ever used by the British Army, and 3,853 were produced between 1942 and 1945. The SOE didn't make much use of the Welbike, but some of the British airborne troops dropped over Arnhem in September 1944 certainly used their Welbikes for extra mobility, once they'd landed in the Wolfheze, Arnhem and Oosterbeek areas.

Other Station IX inventions were not quite so successful. The Welman one-man submarine had no periscope and proved to be very difficult to manoeuvre. As a result, it was largely dropped from operational usage after just one abortive attack on enemy docks in Bergen, Norway. The Welfreighter was a 37-foot midget submarine, intended for the use of special forces and for coastal reconnaissance. However, the new design never really progressed beyond the testing stage, and the war ended before the submarine could be used operationally.

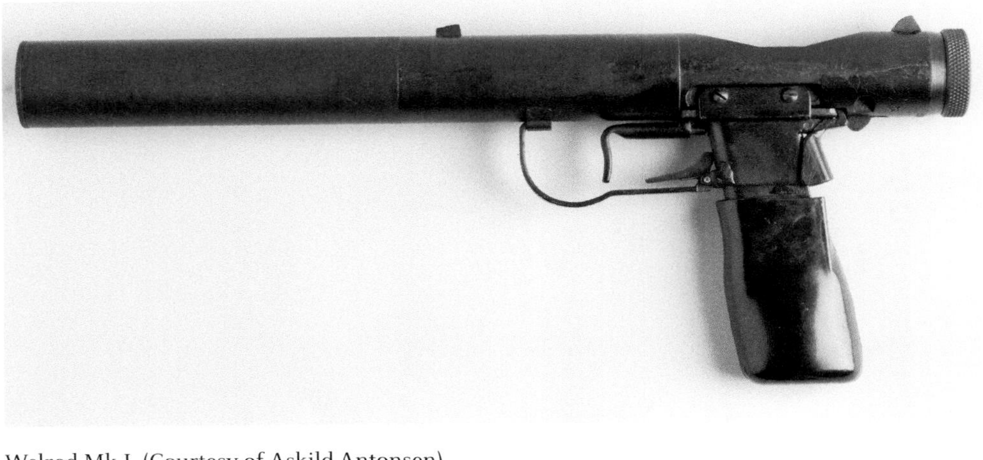

Welrod Mk I. (Courtesy of Askild Antonsen)

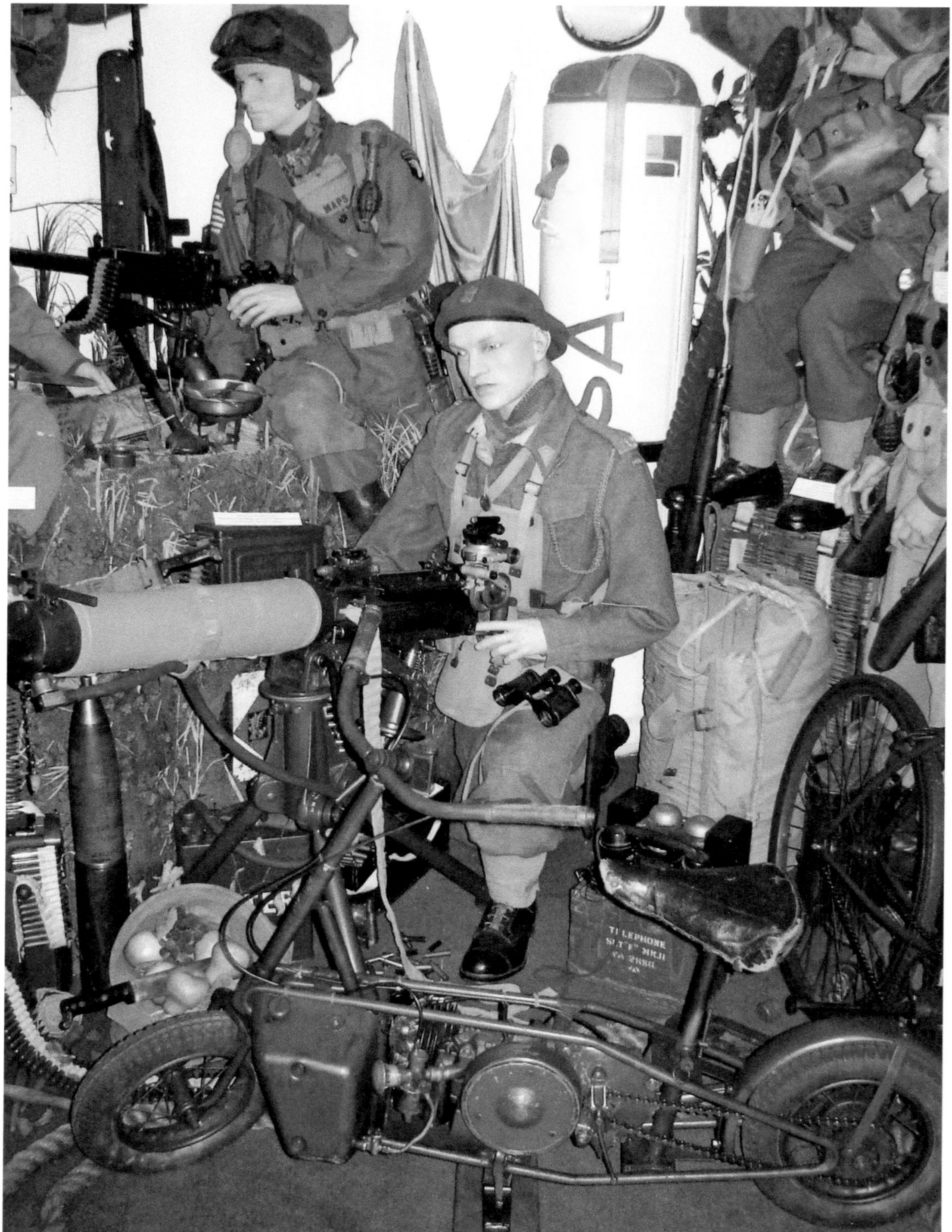

Dutch tableaux of wartime British paratroopers with Welbike. (Courtesy of Jeroen026)

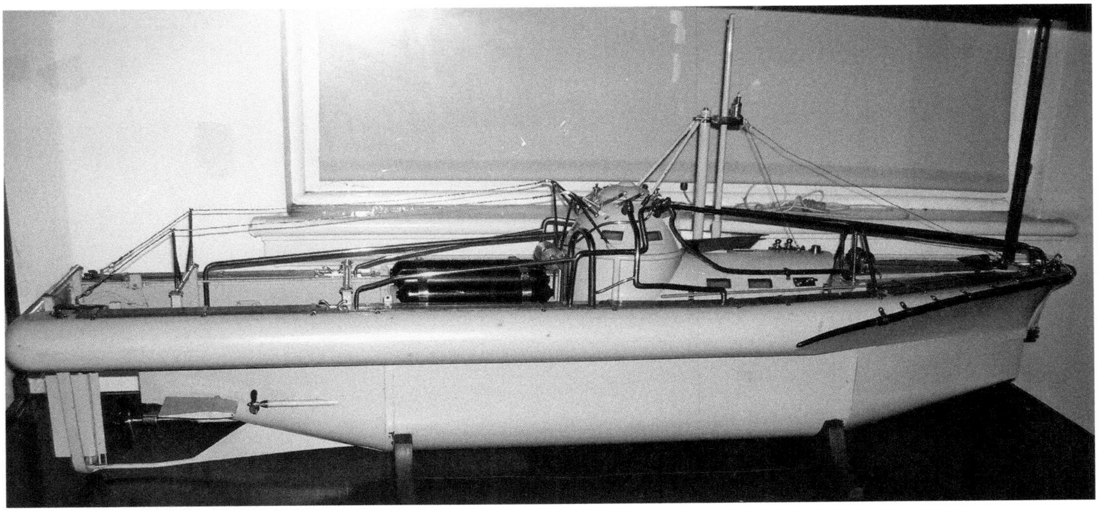

Welfreighter submarine model *c.* 1944, National Maritime Museum. (Courtesy of Remi Kaupp)

John Dolphin continued to serve in the TA even after the end of the Second World War, and he received the Territorial Decoration for long service in the late 1940s. He continued to be a prolific inventor, securing patents for his new designs until well into the 1960s. Prior to his death in 1973, he had developed battery powered bicycles, which anticipated the arrival of modern mobility scooters. He had also made design improvements to forklift trucks and developed better saddles and frames for bicycles. Many of these post-war engineering developments drew considerable inspiration from Dolphin's wartime work in the cloak-and-dagger world of the SOE.

7. For Valour

Since its institution in 1856, in the immediate aftermath of the Crimean War, the Victoria Cross (VC) has been recognised as the ultimate award for bravery in battle by members of the British armed forces. Very few VCs have been awarded during the nearly 170 years since its inception – 1,355 between 1856 and 2020. Before 1907, the award could only be given to those who had undertaken, and survived, outstanding acts of heroism. However, in 1907, changes were made that ensured that the VC could be awarded posthumously to next of kin for those who had perished while undertaking acts of gallantry and heroism. The Cheshire Regiment's first VC was awarded to Private Thomas Alfred Jones, from Runcorn, for his actions during the Somme campaign of 1916. Thomas (known as 'Todger' Jones throughout most of his life) was older than many of his fellow Tommies in the Cheshire Regiment's 1st Battalion. He was born in 1880 and had already experienced the army as a part-time Volunteer and Territorial prior to 1914. Todger was also a crack shot, winning the Territorial Army Efficiency Medal for his marksmanship in 1912. His wartime service began somewhat less than promisingly when he was fined four days' pay for returning late from home leave at the end of 1914. These early blemishes must have been easily forgotten, however, as a result of Todger's remarkable, almost superhuman,

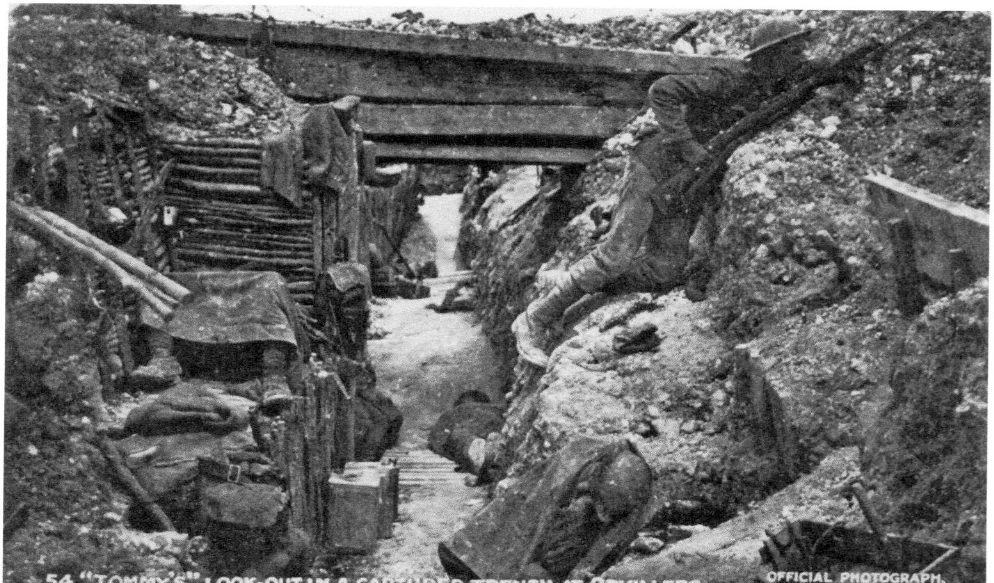

Cheshire Regiment soldiers in captured German trench on the Somme, *Daily Mail* postcard, 1916.

actions at the village of Morval, on the Western Front, on 25 September 1916. Members of the 1st Battalion were plagued by persistent German sniper fire. As a result, Private Jones took matters into his own hands and advanced on his own towards the nearest German positions. He shot the principal German sniper, killed or disabled a number of other enemy soldiers and then leapt into a German trench, where he proceeded to disarm and capture at least 102 German soldiers. Todger then brought at least fifty German prisoners safely back to the Cheshire's lines, through a heavy British artillery barrage.

Jones seems to have led a charmed life during his time at the Front. He was shot through the helmet while capturing the Germans, and his uniform was also shredded in a number of places by bullet holes. On other occasions, he had the heel of his boot shot off, he was blown into the air by an explosion, wounded in the shoulder, and also gassed. Despite all these near brushes with death, Todger was still able to receive his VC in person from George V at a Buckingham Palace investiture in October 1916. On 23 November 1916, Private Jones then travelled to Chester, the home town of the Cheshire Regiment, for a civic reception. Thousands of people lined the streets of the city to greet the war hero, and Chester's mayor and the head of Western Command both gave speeches praising Todger at Chester Castle. After receiving a great many gifts, Private Jones VC returned to active service, and in September 1918 he was awarded another medal for bravery – the Distinguished Conduct Medal – for repeatedly rushing through heavy German artillery fire with vital messages during fighting at Beugny.

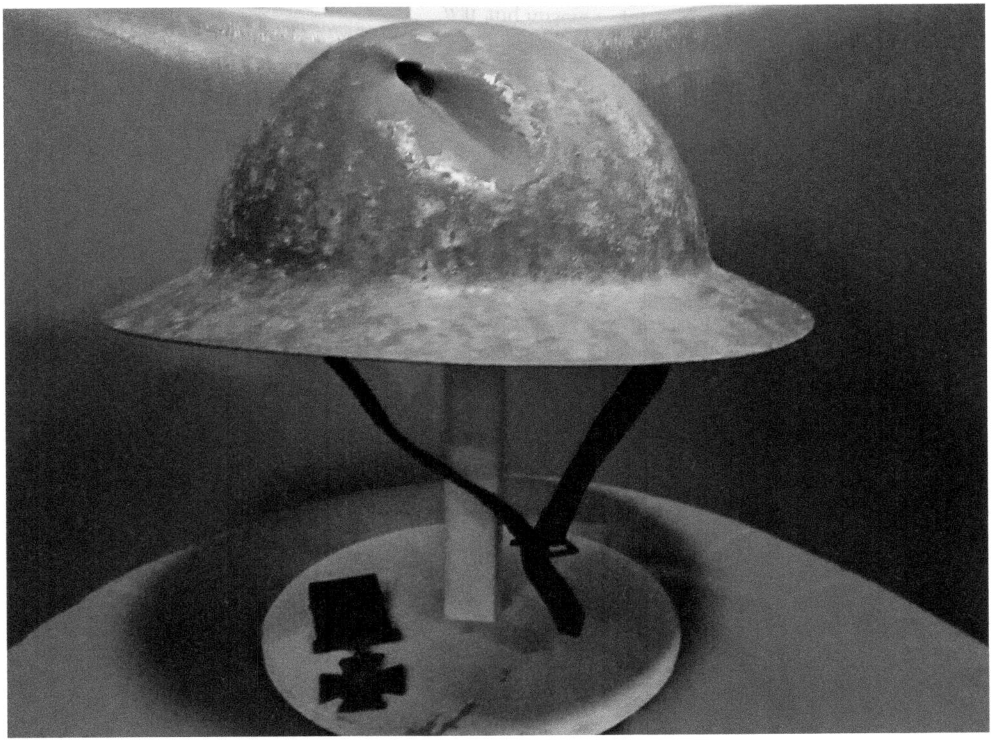

Thomas Jones' helmet, with bullet hole. (© Cheshire Military Museum)

Todger Jones VC, DCM left the army in 1919 and returned to his old job as an engineering fitter at Runcorn's Salt Union Works. He remained an engineering fitter for the next thirty years, and finally passed away in 1956. For most of his life Thomas Jones seems to have been a modest and unassuming man, who never really sought promotion or advancement in either military or civilian life. On the battlefield, however, T. A. Jones was clearly in his element – an unstoppable martial phenomenon, able to think clearly, shoot straight and surmount incredible dangers and challenges.

Hugh Colvin, born in Burnley in 1887, was the Cheshire Regiment's second recipient of Britain's greatest medal for bravery in battle. In September 1917, Second Lieutenant Colvin of the 9th Battalion of the Cheshire Regiment was involved in a desperate battle against German forces, just east of Ypres on the Western Front. The details of the actions for which Colvin won the VC are very similar, in some ways, to those for which Private Jones was decorated in 1916. During an attack on German defences, virtually all of Colvin's officer colleagues were killed or wounded. Colvin was left to take control of two companies of men, and as a result of the leadership he exhibited, the assault on German defensive positions was continued, despite heavy casualties. The second lieutenant from Burnley appears to have leapt into a minimum of two German dugouts, either on his own or with one or two colleagues, and personally taken over fifty German prisoners. Colvin finished the day by single-handedly setting up the regiment's barbed wire defences, in front of their new positions, despite heavy and sustained German sniper fire. On 10

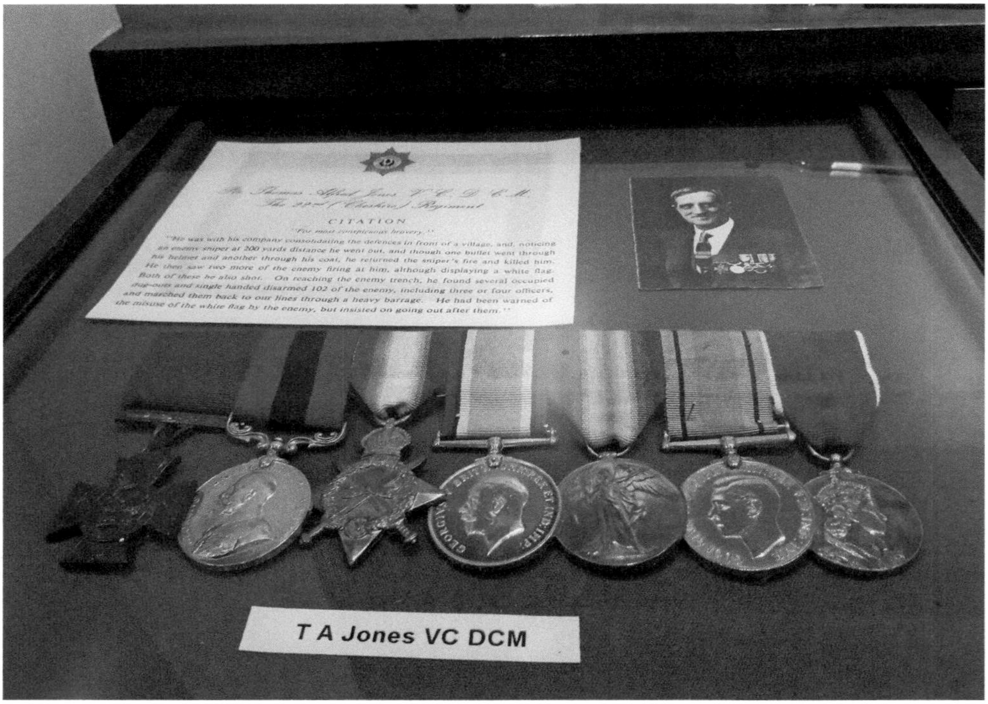

Thomas Jones, VC (extreme left) and medal set. (© Cheshire Military Museum)

November 1917, Colvin was presented with his VC by George V at Buckingham Palace. In December, Colvin travelled to Chester for a civic reception hosted by the city's mayor, the general in charge of Western Command, and the county's chief constable. Crowds lined the streets of Chester (as they had done for T. A. Jones) during a series of events planned at the Eastgate, the Town Hall, and at Chester Castle. Colvin also enjoyed dinner with officers of the Cheshire Regiment (a privilege denied to Todger Jones presumably because of his lack of rank).

In many ways, Jones and Colvin were very different characters. Hugh Colvin, unlike Jones, was a full-time career soldier, who first enlisted in the Royal Irish Hussars in 1908. Colvin also rose through the ranks, unlike Jones. At the onset of war, Colvin was a lance-corporal, but then received a commission as a second-lieutenant in the Cheshire Regiment's 9th Battalion. After the award of his VC, Hugh Colvin became a full lieutenant and a company commander. He stayed in the army after the end of the war and rose to the rank of captain before retiring in 1935. In 1938, he returned to the colours temporarily, as a major in charge of army recruitment in Chester, before finally retiring for good in 1947. Hugh Colvin VC then returned to live with his family in Northern Ireland, where he passed away in 1962.

Although Thomas Jones and Hugh Colvin had close connections to Chester, via the Cheshire Regiment, neither man was born in the city. Leonard Chevalier Cheshire VC, however, who was one of the great heroes of RAF Bomber Command during the

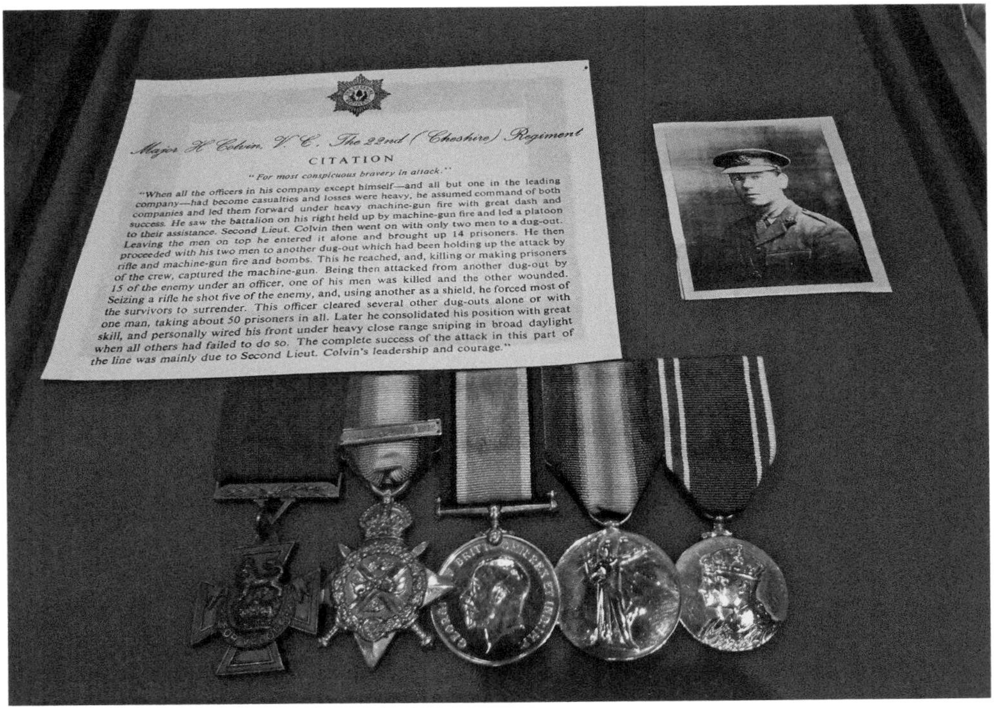

Hugh Colvin's VC (extreme left) and medal set. (© Cheshire Military Museum)

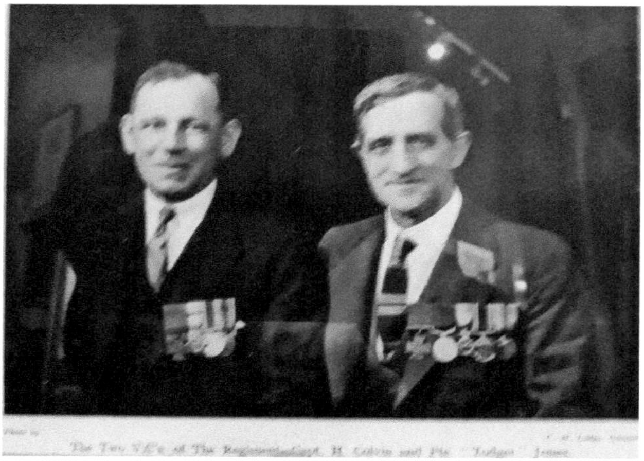

Hugh Colvin (left) and Thomas Jones. (© Cheshire Military Museum)

Second World War, was actually born in Chester, in 1917, and had close ties with both the city and the county of Cheshire that stretched back for generations. Leonard's father had been an officer in the Cheshire Regiment, and then a pilot in the Royal Flying Corps. Leonard himself joined the Oxford University Air Squadron while studying for a degree in jurisprudence. He then went on to have a stellar career in RAF Bomber Command during the Second World War, becoming its youngest wing commander and flying over a hundred missions over German occupied Europe. Cheshire was awarded the VC in September 1944 not really just for one outstandingly brave action, but rather for his sustained active service, combined with his leadership qualities, over a period of four years, between 1940 and 1944. He flew on every kind of raid, from saturation night-time bombing missions over Berlin and Cologne to low-level attacks on strategic rail tunnels, such as that at Saumir in the Loire valley on 8 June 1944. His last operational mission took place on 6 July 1944 and was against a German V-weapon site at Mimoyecques. As a wing commander, Leonard Cheshire was a more nuanced character than is sometimes believed. He was quietly spoken and took the trouble to know everyone under his command – from cooks to pilots. He could, however, be ruthless when required. Bomber Command casualties during the Second World War were enormous (over 57,000 were killed in action) and not all aircrews could cope with the enormous strain of risking their lives on a daily basis in the night skies above occupied Europe. In an era before post-traumatic stress disorder (PTSD) and other psychological disorders were really recognised, Bomber Command personnel who broke down under the strain of constant action were simply said to be 'lacking moral fibre (LMF)' and quickly moved away from their RAF stations. Leonard Cheshire was certainly among those commanders who shared the prejudices of the time, and he ruthlessly expunged the 'contagion' of LMF from the crews under his command. Cheshire was also on close terms with Sir Arthur Harris, head of RAF Bomber Command, and one of the principal architects of the policy of area bombing, which led to the wholesale devastation of German cities, and the killing of hundreds of thousands of German civilians. Both men seemed to share the rather brutal basic philosophy that killing as many Germans as quickly as possible was absolutely necessary in order to win the war.

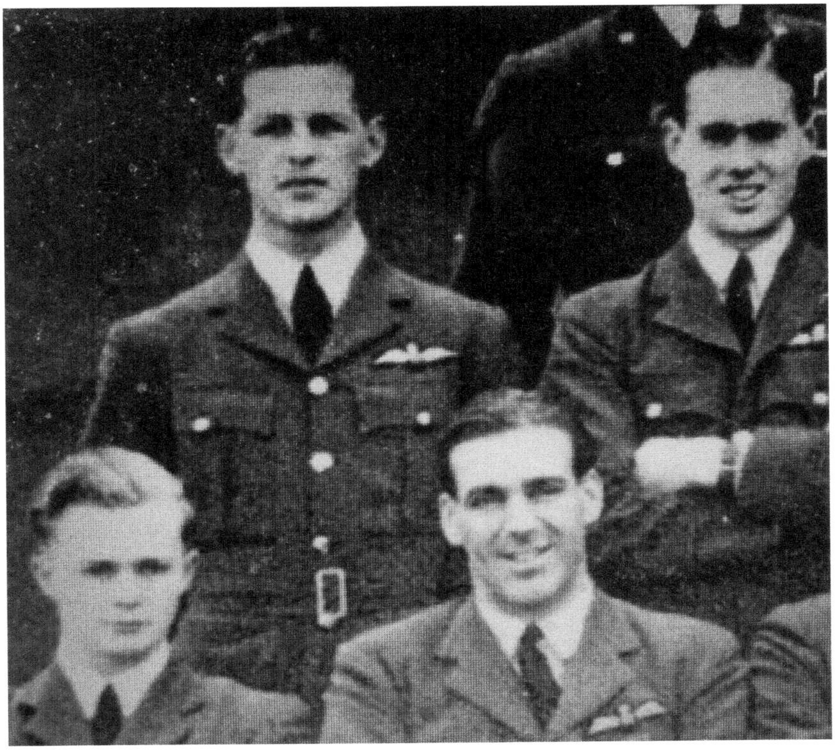

A young Leonard Cheshire (second row, far right), 102 Squadron, July 1940. (© Spartacus Educational)

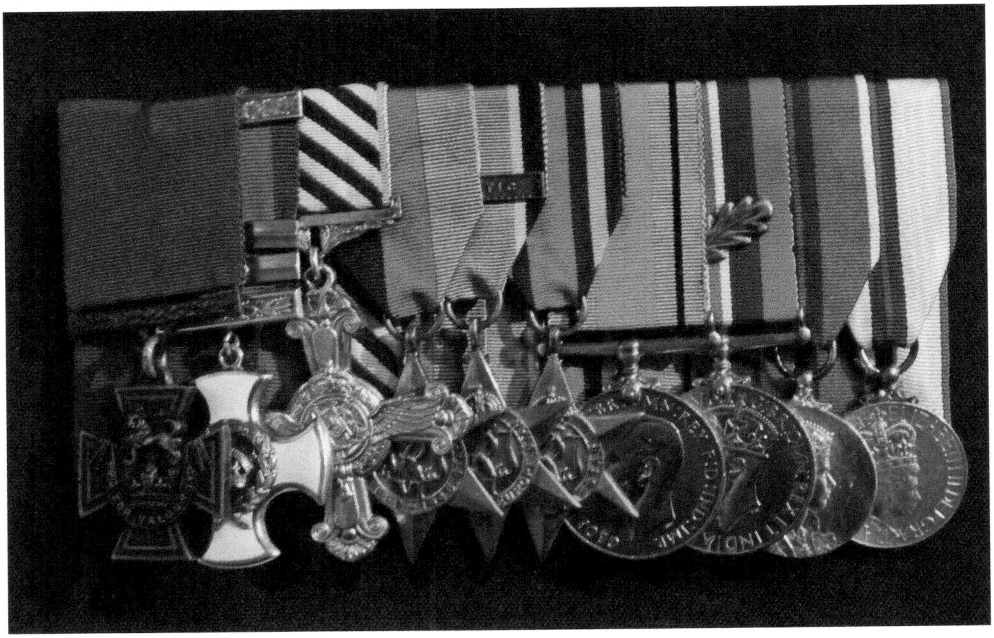

Leonard Cheshire's medals (VC extreme left). (Courtesy of Woody)

On 9 August 1945, Cheshire was the official British observer when the Americans dropped the atomic bomb on the Japanese city of Nagasaki. The experience had a profound effect on Cheshire, who later became a member of the Campaign for Nuclear Disarmament (CND). In 1948, the distinguished RAF war hero used his home in Liss, Hampshire, to accommodate a homeless, terminally ill ex-serviceman. From this single act of compassion and kindness grew the idea for the Leonard Cheshire Foundation, which by 2007 was accommodating disabled veterans and other people in homes spread across fifty-two countries. By the time of his death in 1992, Leonard Cheshire's legacy had moved beyond the purely military to encompass social policy and charitable causes across the world.

The monumental achievements of Chester-born Leonard Cheshire have rather served to obscure the fact that the city of Chester has produced other martial heroes of great distinction. Kenneth Muir, for example, was born in Chester in March 1912. He was born into a notable military family. Kenneth's father had been called Garnet Wolseley Muir, in honour of Sir Garnet Wolseley, the famous major-general of the Victorian era. Garnet Muir had then gone on to become commanding officer of the legendary Argyll and Sutherland Highlanders infantry regiment. His son, Kenneth, seems to have been destined to follow in his father's footsteps from a very early age. In 1932, Kenneth Muir was commissioned as a lieutenant in the Argyll and Sutherland Highlanders, and during the 1930s, he spent much time fighting on the violent North West Frontier of India. During the Second World War, he saw service in the Sudan, North Africa, Italy, France and Germany. Although he had some staff jobs during this period, well away from the front line, he still saw enough active service to receive the honour of being mentioned in dispatches. It was in the Korean War, rather than the Second World War, that Kenneth Muir's courage as a soldier and, as a commander, was to be truly revealed. The south-eastern Asia country of Korea had been occupied by Japan since 1910. Following Japan's total defeat in 1945, the north part of Korea had been made into a communist state under Kim Il Sung, and south of the 38th parallel, a democratic state under Syngman Rhee had been created. On 25 June 1950, the communist north invaded the south, and British troops were sent to support Rhee's country (as part of a United Nations force commanded by the Americans). Chester-born Kenneth Muir and the Argyll and Sutherland Highlanders were among the very first British troops to begin fighting on the Korean Peninsula, as part of what soon became known as the 27th (Commonwealth) Brigade. North Korean troops quickly occupied most of the south, apart from a small area around the south-eastern port of Pusan. In September 1950, UN forces, including the 27th Brigade, began to push outwards from this so-called Pusan Pocket, and on 23 September 1950 the Argyll and Sutherland Highlanders became involved in a desperate battle for the strategically vital Hill 282, in the province of Seongju. Major Muir, who was second-in-command of the Highlanders, first became personally involved during the effort to extricate casualties from Hill 282. He led stretcher parties onto the hill at a time when the Scottish soldiers were being overwhelmed by counter-attacking North Koreans. Muir led the fight against the attackers, and called in US airstrikes to assist his men. Tragically, the Americans hit their allies rather than the North Koreans, in one of the first and worst examples of 'friendly fire' in the Korean War. Muir and his men had little option but to retire some way down the hill. It was at this point that Major Muir organised and led a counter-attack involving thirty men of all ranks, which again took the summit of Hill 282, despite overwhelming odds. Ammunition was running low, however, and it was here, at the head of his men, and firing a 2-inch mortar, that Kenneth Muir was cut down and killed by enemy fire. As a result of his actions, Muir was posthumously awarded the Victoria Cross, and he was also given the Distinguished Service Order (DSO) by the Americans. Kenneth Muir's parents received their son's VC from George VI in person during a 1951 Buckingham Palace ceremony. Muir's father, Garnett Wolseley Muir, never really recovered from the death of his son on Hill 282, and in 1954, obviously burdened by grief and sadness, he took his own life. Garnett Muir, just as much as his son Kenneth, was a sad casualty of the Korean War.

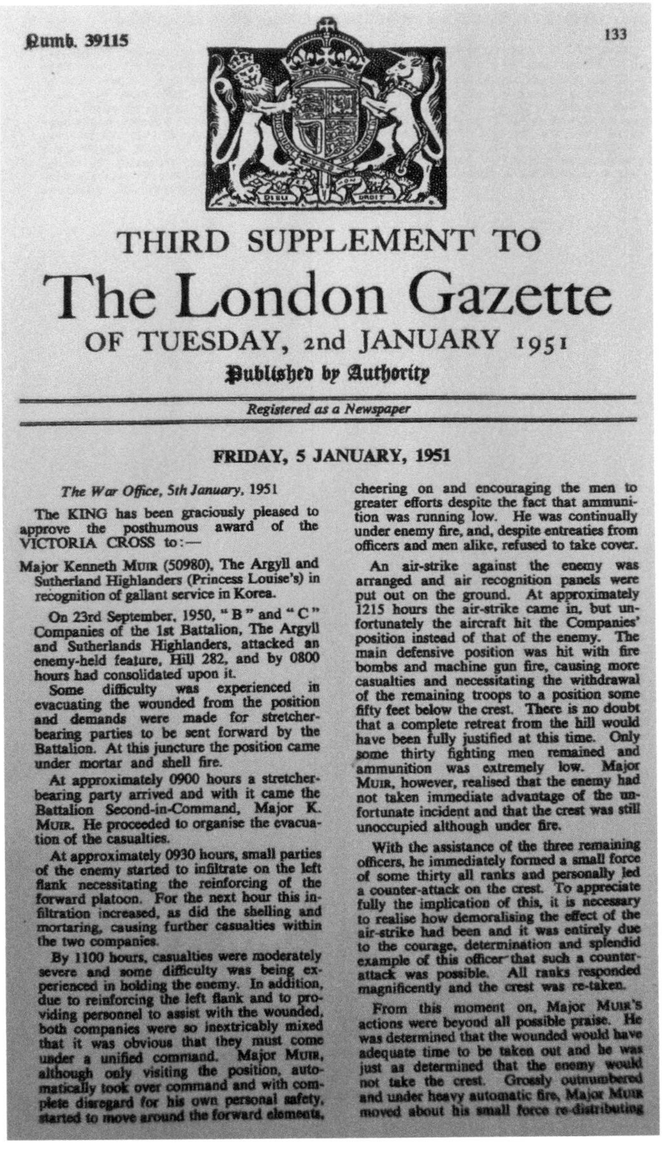

Numb. 39115 133

THIRD SUPPLEMENT TO

The London Gazette

OF TUESDAY, 2nd JANUARY 1951

Published by Authority

Registered as a Newspaper

FRIDAY, 5 JANUARY, 1951

The War Office, 5th January, 1951

The KING has been graciously pleased to approve the posthumous award of the VICTORIA CROSS to:—

Major Kenneth MUIR (50980), The Argyll and Sutherland Highlanders (Princess Louise's) in recognition of gallant service in Korea.

On 23rd September, 1950, "B" and "C" Companies of the 1st Battalion, The Argyll and Sutherlands Highlanders, attacked an enemy-held feature, Hill 282, and by 0800 hours had consolidated upon it.

Some difficulty was experienced in evacuating the wounded from the position and demands were made for stretcher-bearing parties to be sent forward by the Battalion. At this juncture the position came under mortar and shell fire.

At approximately 0900 hours a stretcher-bearing party arrived and with it came the Battalion Second-in-Command, Major K. MUIR. He proceeded to organise the evacuation of the casualties.

At approximately 0930 hours, small parties of the enemy started to infiltrate on the left flank necessitating the reinforcing of the forward platoon. For the next hour this infiltration increased, as did the shelling and mortaring, causing further casualties within the two companies.

By 1100 hours, casualties were moderately severe and some difficulty was being experienced in holding the enemy. In addition, due to reinforcing the left flank and to providing personnel to assist with the wounded, both companies were so inextricably mixed that it was obvious that they must come under a unified command. Major MUIR, although only visiting the position, automatically took over command and with complete disregard for his own personal safety, started to move around the forward elements, cheering on and encouraging the men to greater efforts despite the fact that ammunition was running low. He was continually under enemy fire, and, despite entreaties from officers and men alike, refused to take cover.

An air-strike against the enemy was arranged and air recognition panels were put out on the ground. At approximately 1215 hours the air-strike came in, but unfortunately the aircraft hit the Companies' position instead of that of the enemy. The main defensive position was hit with fire bombs and machine gun fire, causing more casualties and necessitating the withdrawal of the remaining troops to a position some fifty feet below the crest. There is no doubt that a complete retreat from the hill would have been fully justified at this time. Only some thirty fighting men remained and ammunition was extremely low. Major MUIR, however, realised that the enemy had not taken immediate advantage of the unfortunate incident and that the crest was still unoccupied although under fire.

With the assistance of the three remaining officers, he immediately formed a small force of some thirty all ranks and personally led a counter-attack on the crest. To appreciate fully the implication of this, it is necessary to realise how demoralising the effect of the air-strike had been and it was entirely due to the courage, determination and splendid example of this officer that such a counter-attack was possible. All ranks responded magnificently and the crest was re-taken.

From this moment on, Major MUIR's actions were beyond all possible praise. He was determined that the wounded would have adequate time to be taken out and he was just as determined that the enemy would not take the crest. Grossly outnumbered and under heavy automatic fire, Major MUIR moved about his small force re-distributing

London Gazette's official announcement of Kenneth Muir's VC.

8. Memorials and Monuments

The city of Chester's long military heritage is clearly shown by its wide array of memorials and monuments, some of which stretch back nearly 2,000 years. Ancient Deva's resident Valeria Victrix Legion left behind many traces of its presence, both in the settlement of Deva and throughout the wider province of Britannia. Chester's Grosvenor Museum, for example, still retains the tombstone of Caecilius Avatis among its collection of Roman exhibits. Caecilius was a Roman soldier who served for fifteen years as an optio in the Deva-based XXth Legion. The optio was a key figure in the ancient Roman army, acting as the second-in-command to a centurion and occupying a position roughly analogous to that of a lieutenant in a modern army.

Just outside the entrance to Chester Castle, and in the middle of the Grosvenor Street roundabout, lie two reminders of a more recent conflict – the Napoleonic Wars. The 23-foot-high equestrian statue of Field Marshall Sir Stapleton Cotton, situated just outside the castle car park, is one of Chester's most overlooked yet impressive military monuments. The 11-foot-high bronze statue of Cotton, which stands on a 12-foot pedestal made of Cornish granite, was created in 1865 by the Italian-born French sculptor Carlo Marochetti. The monument commemorates the achievements of one of the great military figures of the late Georgian and early Victorian period. Cotton, born in 1773, became a distinguished

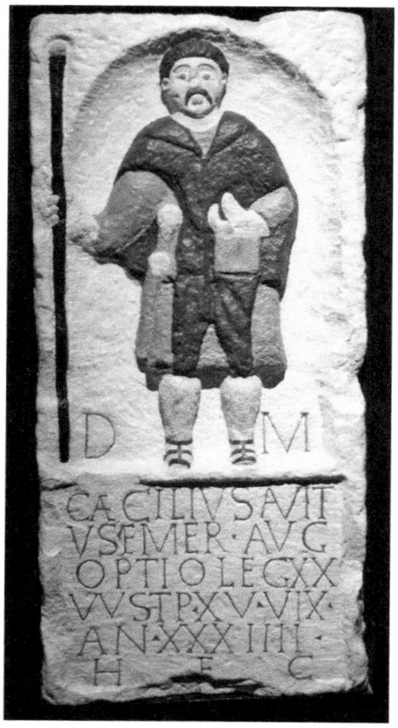

Tombstone of Caecilius Avitus. (Courtesy of Wolfgang Sauber)

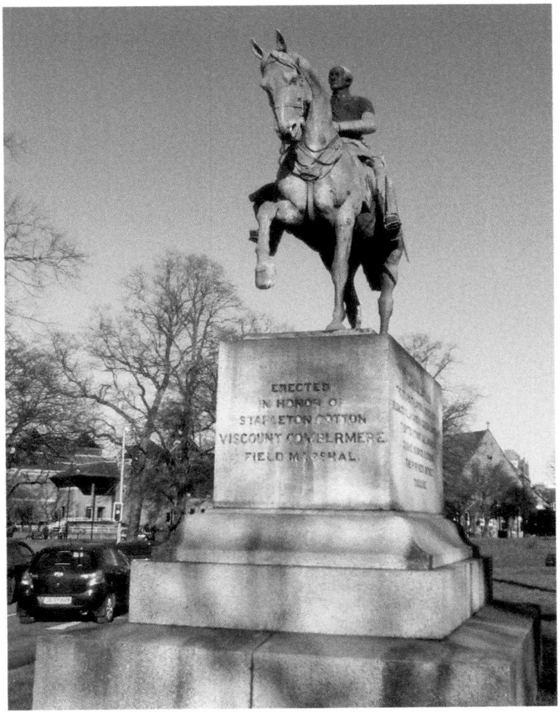

Front view of the Stapleton Cotton statue.

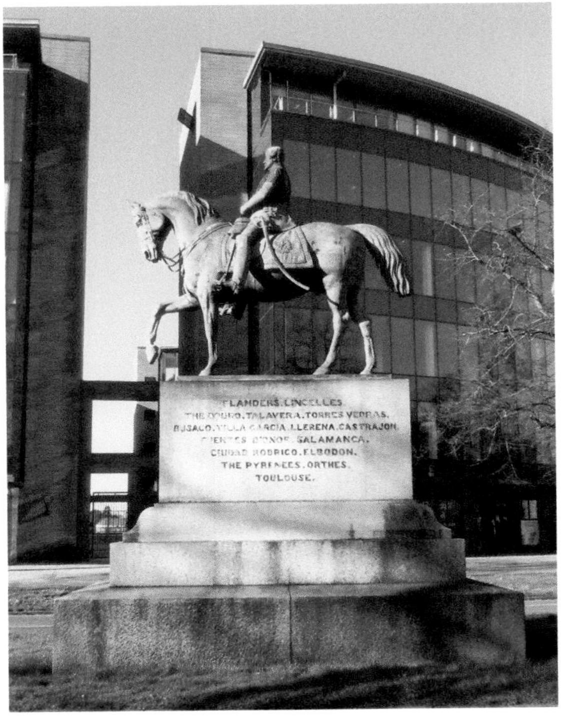

Side view of the Cotton statue.

army officer who commanded armies in both India and Europe. He also became a friend and confidante of Sir Arthur Wellesley, Duke of Wellington, and commanded Wellesley's British and allied cavalry during the Peninsula War. This war, fought by Britain in order to expel Napoleon's armies from Portugal and Spain, really marked the highpoint of Cotton's career. Wellesley was deeply suspicious of cavalry forces because he believed them to be reckless and ill-disciplined. Cotton, however, kept the British cavalry well under control, and used them very effectively in a number of key battles during the Peninsula campaign. He missed the Battle of Waterloo, much to Wellington's disappointment, but his career still prospered once the Napoleonic Wars were at an end. Stapleton Cotton inherited the Combermere Abbey estate (roughly 26 miles south of Chester) in 1809, and in 1825 he was given the title of Viscount Combermere, as a reward for leading British forces – including the 22nd Cheshire's – in the capture of the supposedly impregnable Indian fortress of Bhurtpore. Cotton retired from active service in 1830 and was appointed to the rank of field marshall in 1856. Marochetti's Chester statue of this now largely forgotten British general was officially unveiled in 1865, which was also the year of Cotton's death. In 2020, 155 years later, the statue still remains at the same Chester location and is judged to be a Grade II listed monument of 'some national importance'.

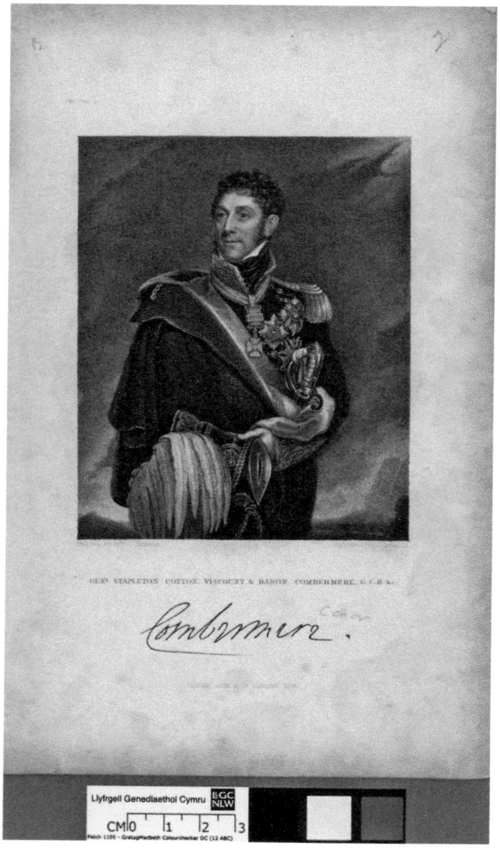

Stapleton Cotton, by Joseph Jenkins, 1839.
(© National Library of Wales)

Close by Cotton's statue, there is another relatively unknown link to the far-off times of the Peninsula War. Right in the middle of the Grosvenor Street roundabout lies the solitary tombstone of Thomas Gould, a former soldier with the 52nd (Oxfordshire) Regiment of Foot, who died in Chester in November 1865 at the age of seventy-two and was buried in the churchyard of St Brigit's Church. The church was pulled down in 1891, and although other people's remains were exhumed and then reinterred at other locations, Gould's tomb was, for some reason, left alone and largely forgotten about. In 1961, however, the sandstone tombstone, shaped like a casket lid, was rediscovered and is now recognised as being a monument of considerable interest. The tomb has a long inscription, which details Gould's military service over forty-six years and his involvement with the 52nd in most of the major battles fought by Wellington in Portugal, Spain and southern France during the period of the Peninsula War. In addition, Gould is also referred to as participating in the Battle of Waterloo. The casket-shaped tomb, with its extensive inscriptions, appears to have been funded by a few of Gould's friends. At first sight, one might think these friends had rather exaggerated the martial exploits of Gould and the 52nd Foot. In reality, though, it appears that the 52nd did indeed play a huge role in the Peninsula fighting, and at Waterloo.

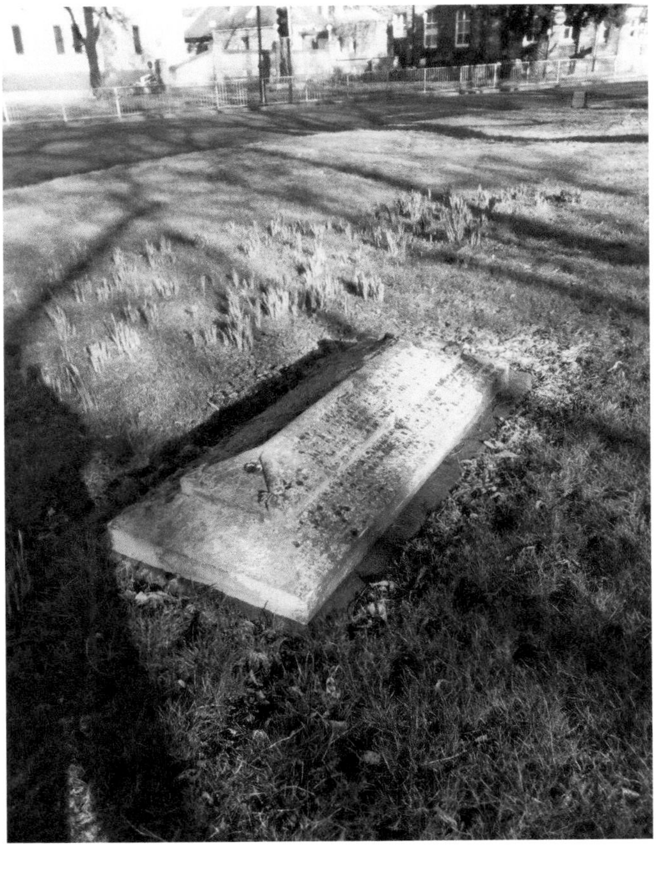

Thomas Gould tombstone.

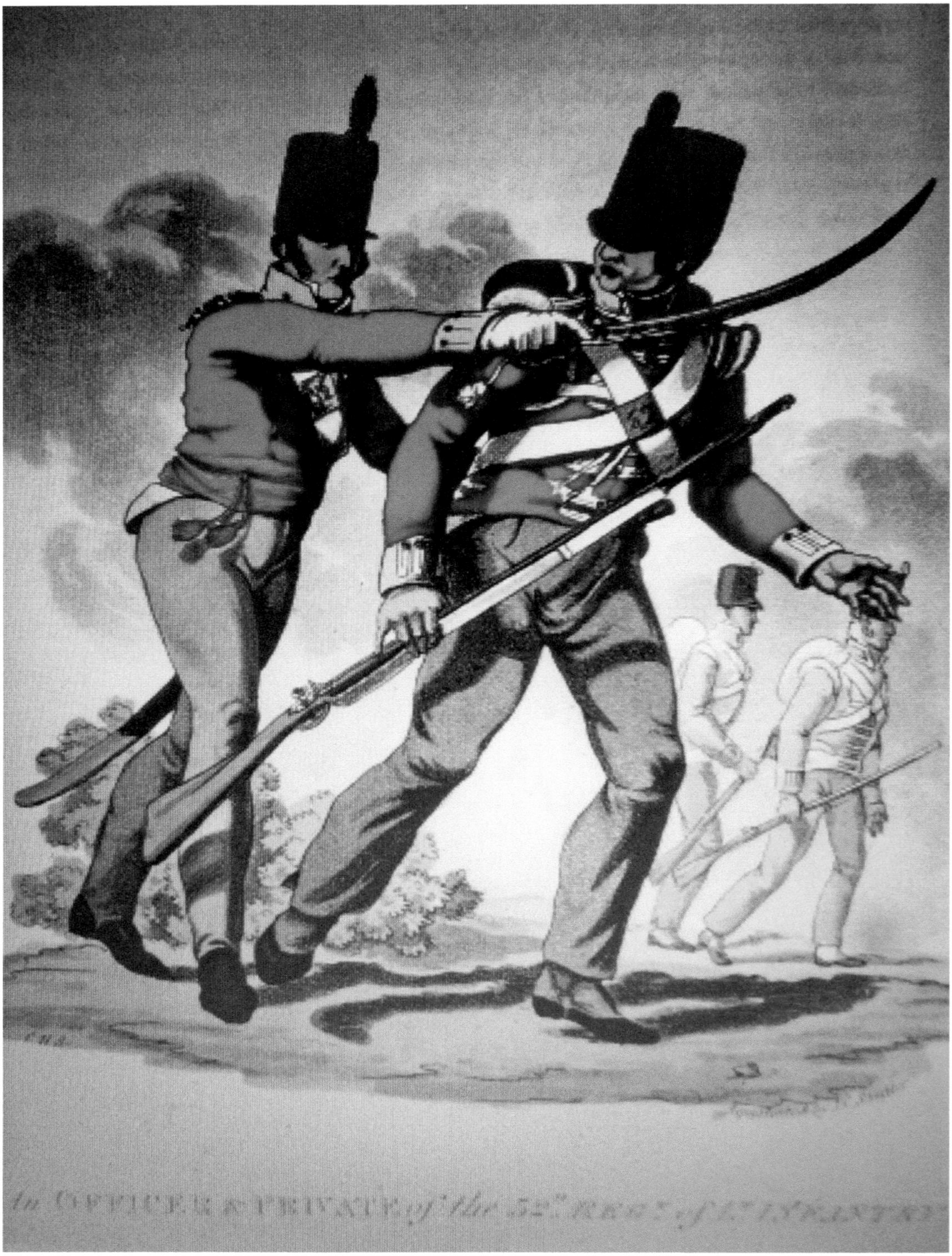

Early nineteenth-century illustration of 52nd Foot officer and private, by J. Stadler.

The 52nd (Oxfordshire) Regiment of Foot was a crack light infantry regiment that acquired an awesome fighting reputation. At the sieges of Badajoz and Cuidad Rodrigo in 1812, the 52nd were among the very first soldiers to storm the French defences, and they suffered very heavy casualties as a consequence. At Waterloo the 52nd was the largest British battalion present on the battlefield and they played a major part in defeating the final attack of Napoleon's Imperial Guard. Given the regiment's almost constant presence on the battlefields of western Europe between 1808 and 1815, Thomas Gould was certainly lucky to survive and to have the chance of living out his final days in the relative tranquillity of mid-Victorian Chester.

While the Cotton statue and Gould's tombstone relate to Chester's early nineteenth-century military heritage, nearby Chester Cathedral contains monuments and memorials that reflect the city's close involvement in more recent conflicts. The cathedral's south transept, for example, contains two memorials to soldiers killed in the 1899–1902 Boer War. The white marble memorial designed by Thomas Rudge, and unveiled by Field Marshall Robertson in 1904, contains a particularly evocative list of 119 men of the Cheshire Regiment who died in South Africa during the often-brutal struggle with the Boers. Each name recorded has its own story of service and sacrifice. Most men died of disease, a few were drowned, and at least one man was struck down by a bolt of lightning. Others, however, died as the result of wounds received in battle.

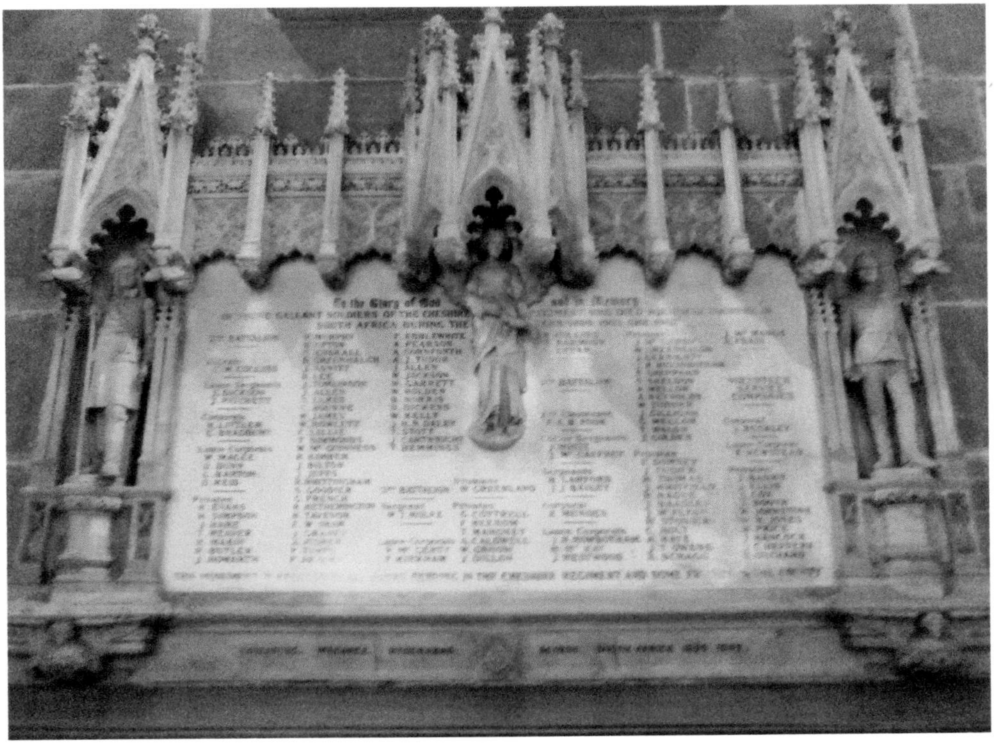

Chester Cathedral Boer War Memorial.

Captain Charles Welman Collins was one of the most distinguished officers recorded on the memorial. He was born in 1872, at No. 6 Waterloo Road, Chester, and went on to serve as a signalling officer in the Cheshire Regiment during the Boer War. He had the unusual distinction of being mentioned in dispatches by both Field Marshall Roberts and Horatio Kitchener, who were the two generals in command of British and Imperial forces during the Boer campaign. Captain Collins certainly saw the brutal side of the war, serving as a member of Colonel Benson's No. 3 Flying Column, which specialised in attacking Boers at night and destroying Boer farms and crops on the high veldt. The Boers certainly feared Benson's force, and took every opportunity to try and destroy it. In November 1901, at the Battle of Bakenlaagte a numerically superior force of mounted Boers, under Louis Botha, surprised Benson's men and came close to annihilating the British column. Only a spirited rearguard action saved the day for the British, and it was during this desperate fighting that Charles Collins was killed.

Chester Cathedral's post-Boer War military memorials and monuments contain much of significance linked to both the First and Second World Wars. The Chester district has a number of impressive war memorials, but the memorial constructed on the green immediately outside Chester Cathedral in 1922 has a particularly poignant history. This cathedral-based memorial was commissioned, like many others, to honour the fallen of the First World War. A maximum fund of £2,000 was allocated to fund the project, and an open competition was launched to find the best and most cost-effective design for the planned memorial. The competition was won by the architects Frederick Crossley and Thomas Rayson, who designed a 32-foot-high memorial cross made of red sandstone, brought from nearby Delamere. The cost of the cross came in well under budget, at £1,540, and was officially unveiled in November 1922 by two Chester mothers, Lydia

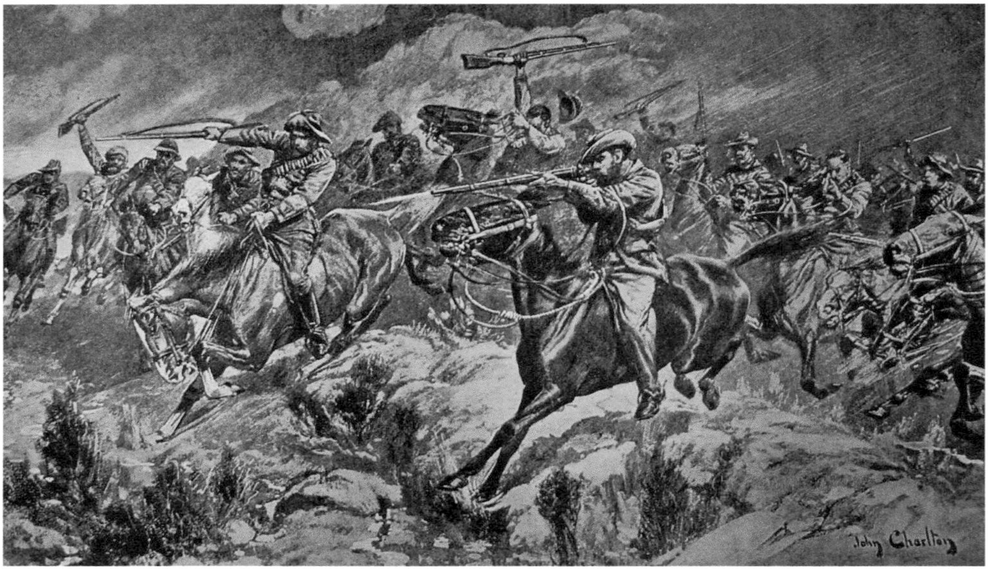

Boer charge at Bakenlaagte, 30 October 1901.

Sheriff-Roberts and Mary Beatty, who had each lost three sons during the war. Mary Beatty had brought up her family in Broughton, and her son Hugh was killed while serving with the Cheshire Regiment on the Western Front in 1916. Another son, Peter, died while serving with the Royal Navy in 1917, and a third son, Richard, died in Egypt in 1918 while serving as a sapper in the Royal Engineers. Within thirteen months of unveiling

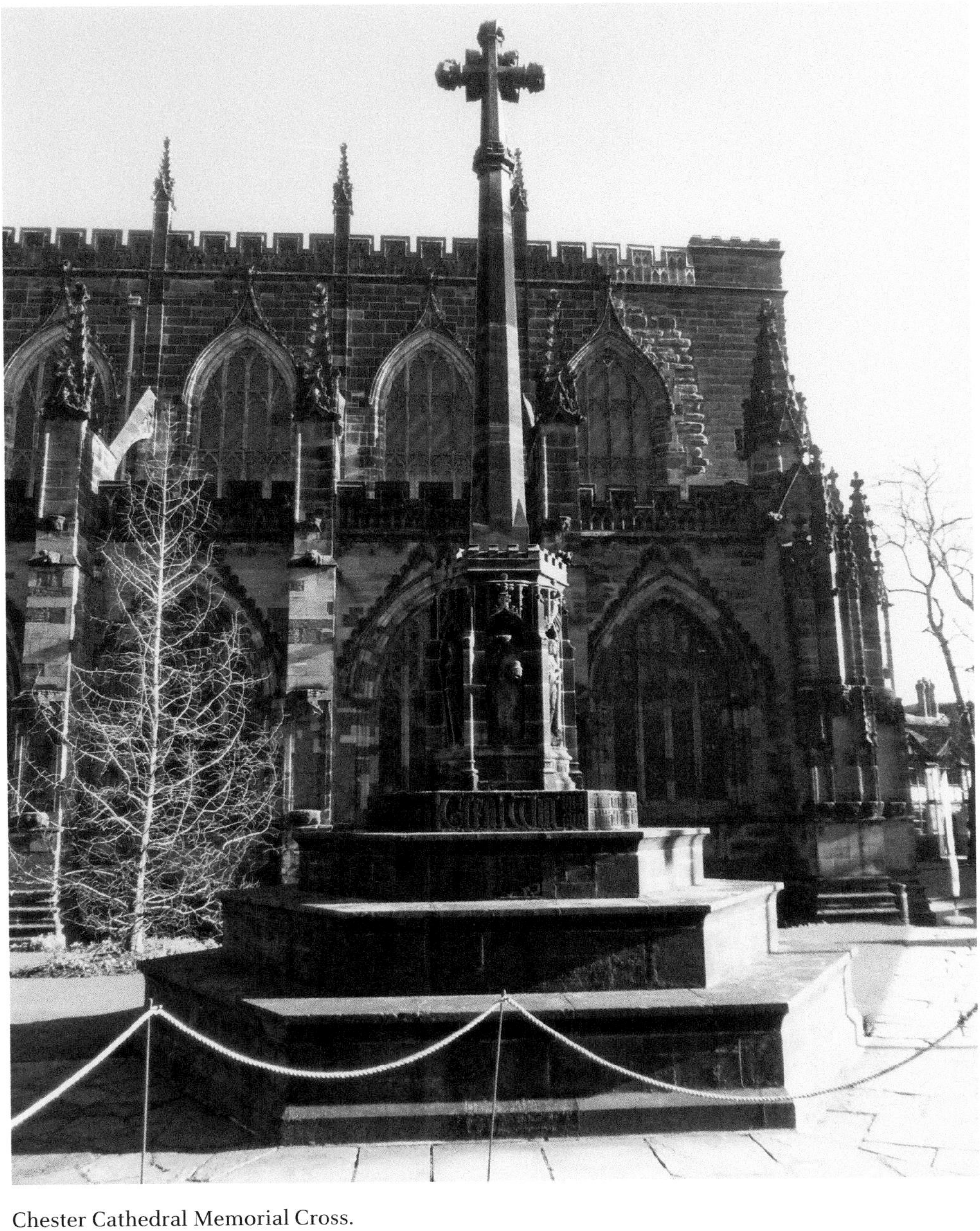

Chester Cathedral Memorial Cross.

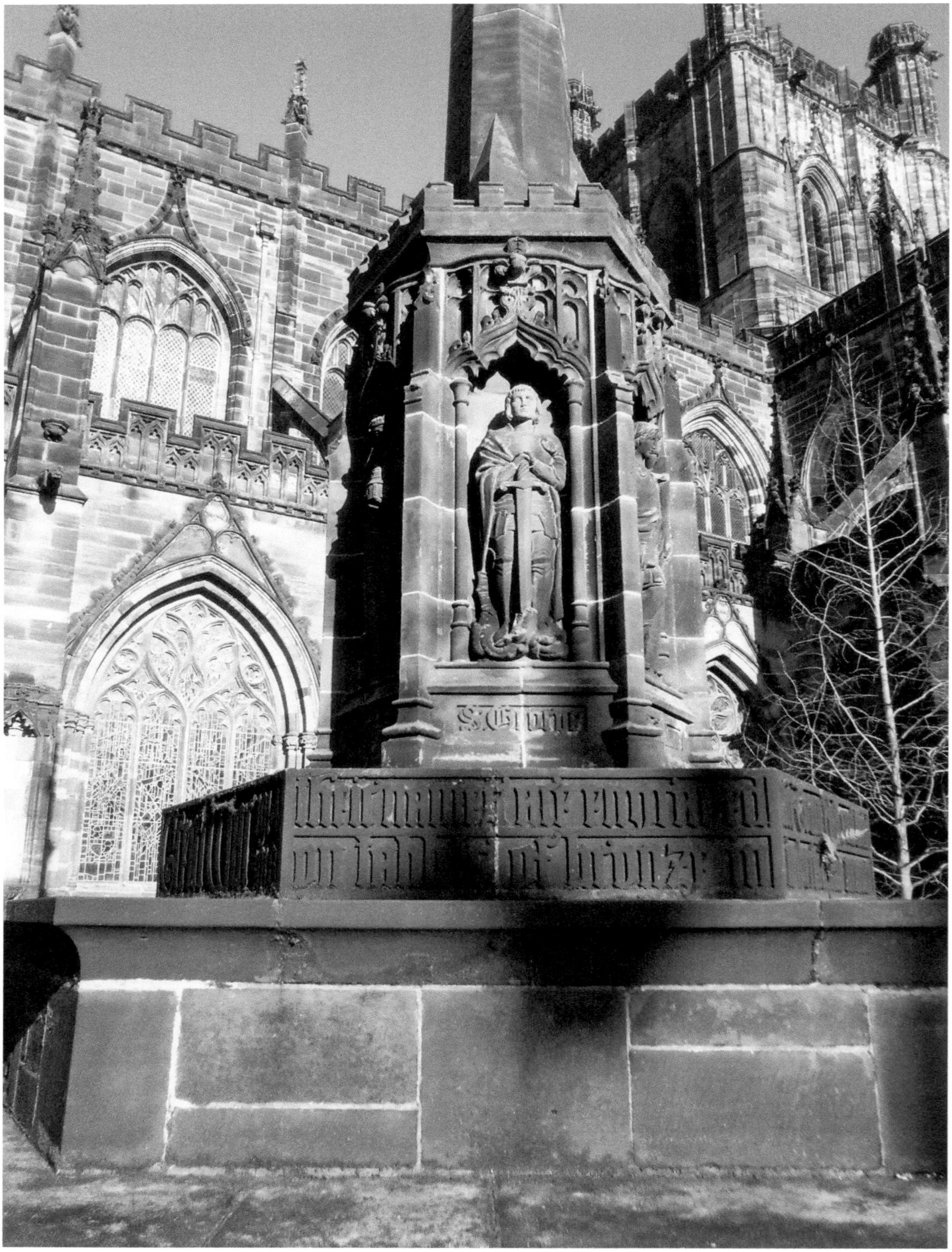

Carved figure of St George from the Memorial Cross.

the new memorial, Mary Beatty, the mother of this devastated family, had passed away, along with her husband, James. The similarly afflicted Sheriff-Roberts family lived in reasonably affluent circumstances at The Gables in Curzon Park, Chester, where Lydia Sheriff-Roberts' husband, John, was a successful wine merchant. By the time Lydia had helped unveil the Chester memorial in 1922, three of her sons had been lost in the First World War killing fields of France and Belgium. Her three eldest sons, Henry, Alan and Frederick, had all been commissioned as officers in the Royal Welsh Fusiliers, and all three were killed between 1916 and 1918. The sons of the Beatty and Sheriff-Roberts families, along with the names of 762 other local men killed in the First World War, were all included in Chester Town Hall's Roll of Honour War Memorial, which was installed inside the council building in 1922. The names of fallen officers are included in two centre panels, with other ranks listed in eight outer panels. The separation of the dead, according to rank, is certainly different from the policy followed in Commonwealth War Graves Commission (CWGC) cemeteries, where the headstones of generals and colonels can lie next to those of private soldiers. Nevertheless, the Town Hall memorial is an impressive and inclusive one, which contains the names of decorated service personnel as well as those few sad cases of men who were 'shot at dawn' for alleged desertion. The memorial also reflects the enormously wide contribution of the city of Chester to the armed forces during the war, with men recorded as serving in a vast array of army regiments, from the

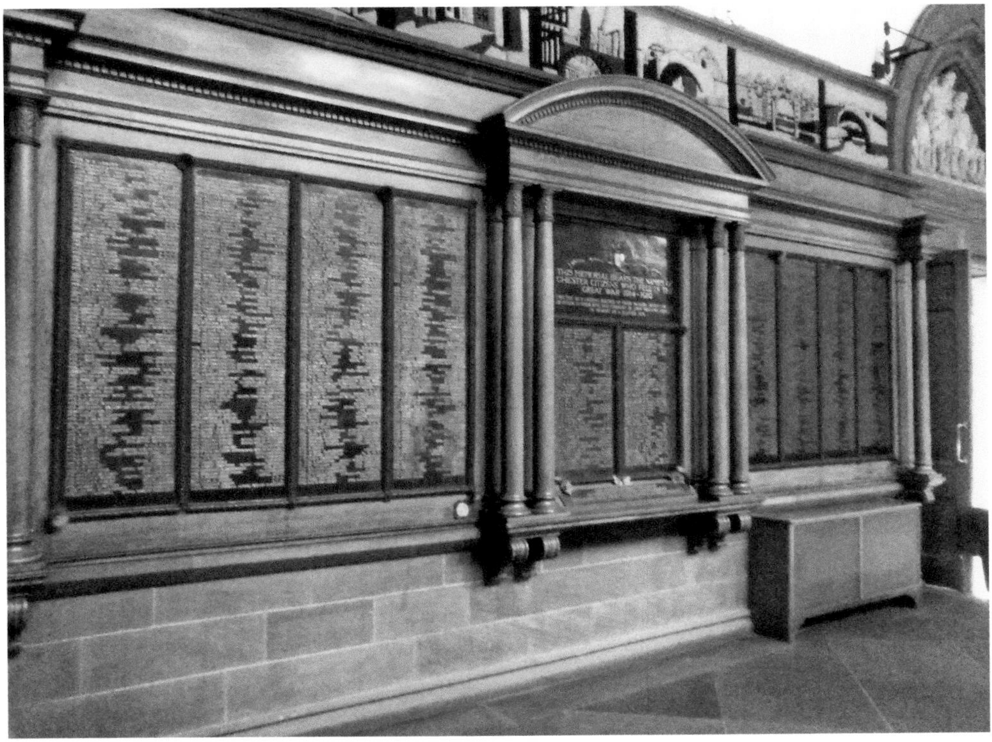

Town Hall Roll of Honour Memorial Panels, Chester Town Hall.

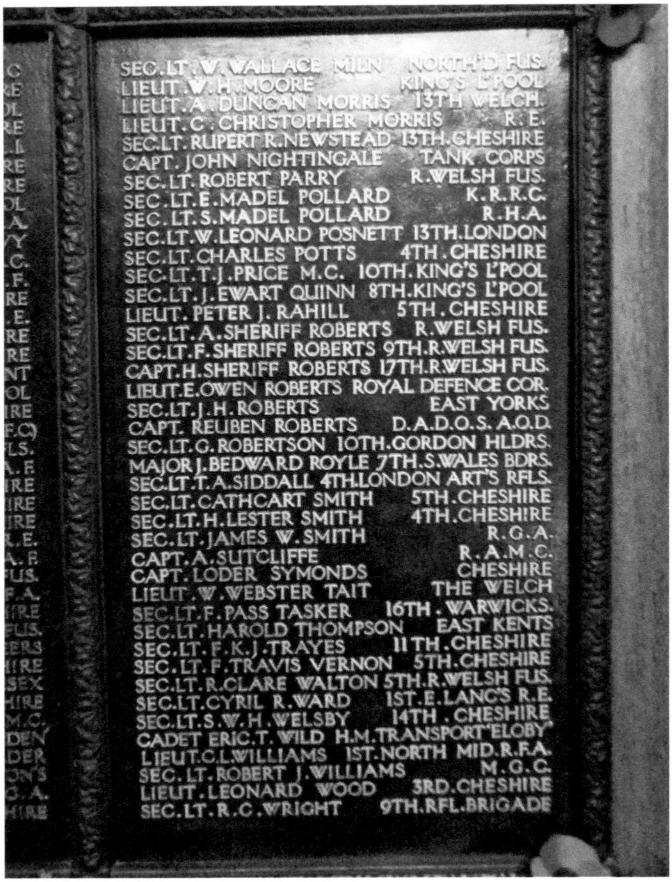

Town Hall panel listing the Sheriff-Roberts brothers.

Coldstream Guards to the Oxfordshire & Buckinghamshire Light Infantry, as well as in the Royal Navy and the RAF.

Chester's memorials and monuments to the fighting forces of the Second World War are even more diverse and wide-ranging than those for the First World War. This reflects the fact that between 1939 and 1945 Chester was the base for Allied forces drawn from all parts of occupied Europe, as well as from America, Canada and the British Commonwealth. As a result, Chester Cathedral has its memorial to Czech soldiers based at nearby Cholmondeley Castle (unveiled in July 1980) and the Town Hall has a memorial to Polish forces. Czech armed forces fatalities were interred in the military section of Overleigh Cemetery in Handbridge, and Polish war dead were buried at Blacon Cemetery. A great many British and Commonwealth RAF casualties were also interred among the pristine white CWGC headstones at Overleigh, Blacon and elsewhere in the Chester district. Indeed, Blacon became the RAF's designated regional cemetery. The numerous RAF dead interred at cemeteries in the area is a reflection of the sheer number of air bases and Operational Training Units (OTUs) dotted around Chester during the Second World War.

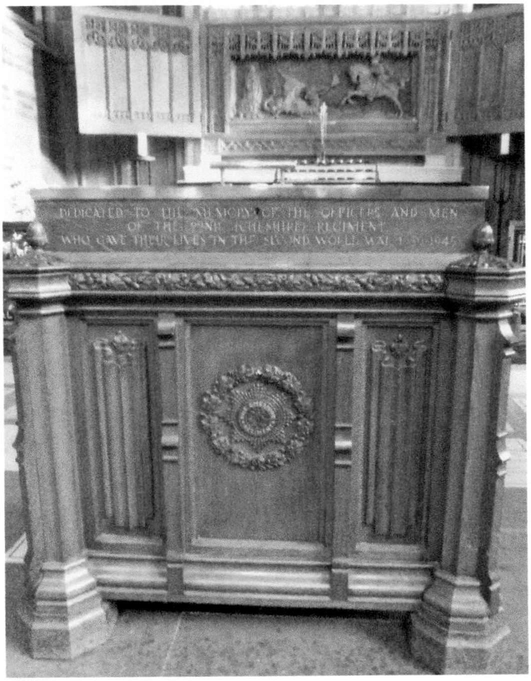

Cheshire Regiment Second World War Memorial, Chester Cathedral.

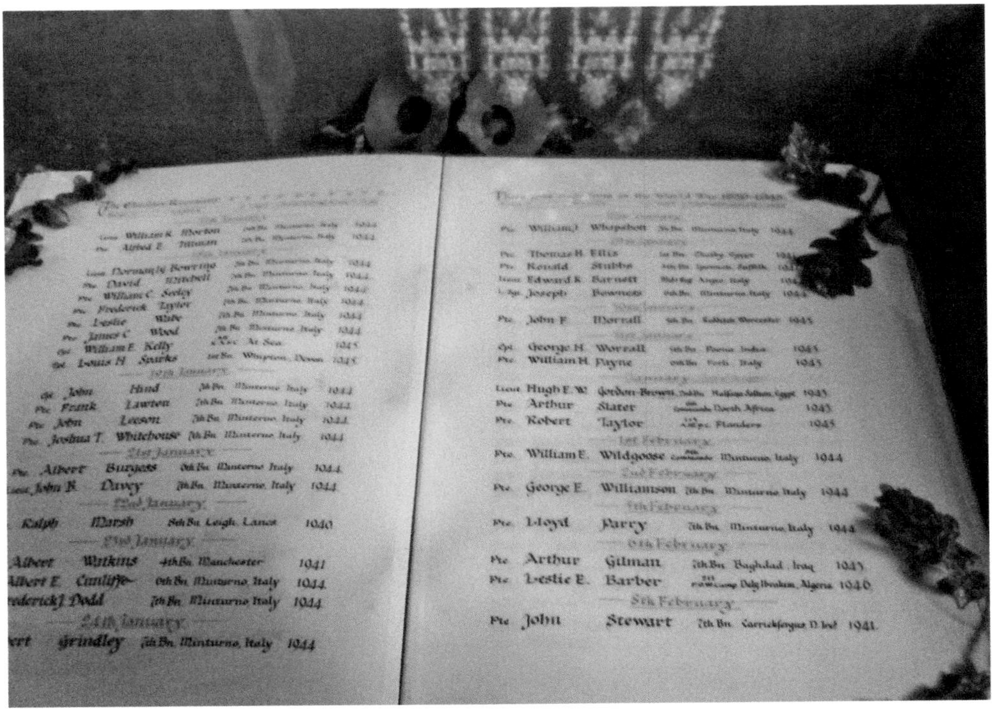

Cheshire Regiment Second World War Book of Remembrance, Chester Cathedral.

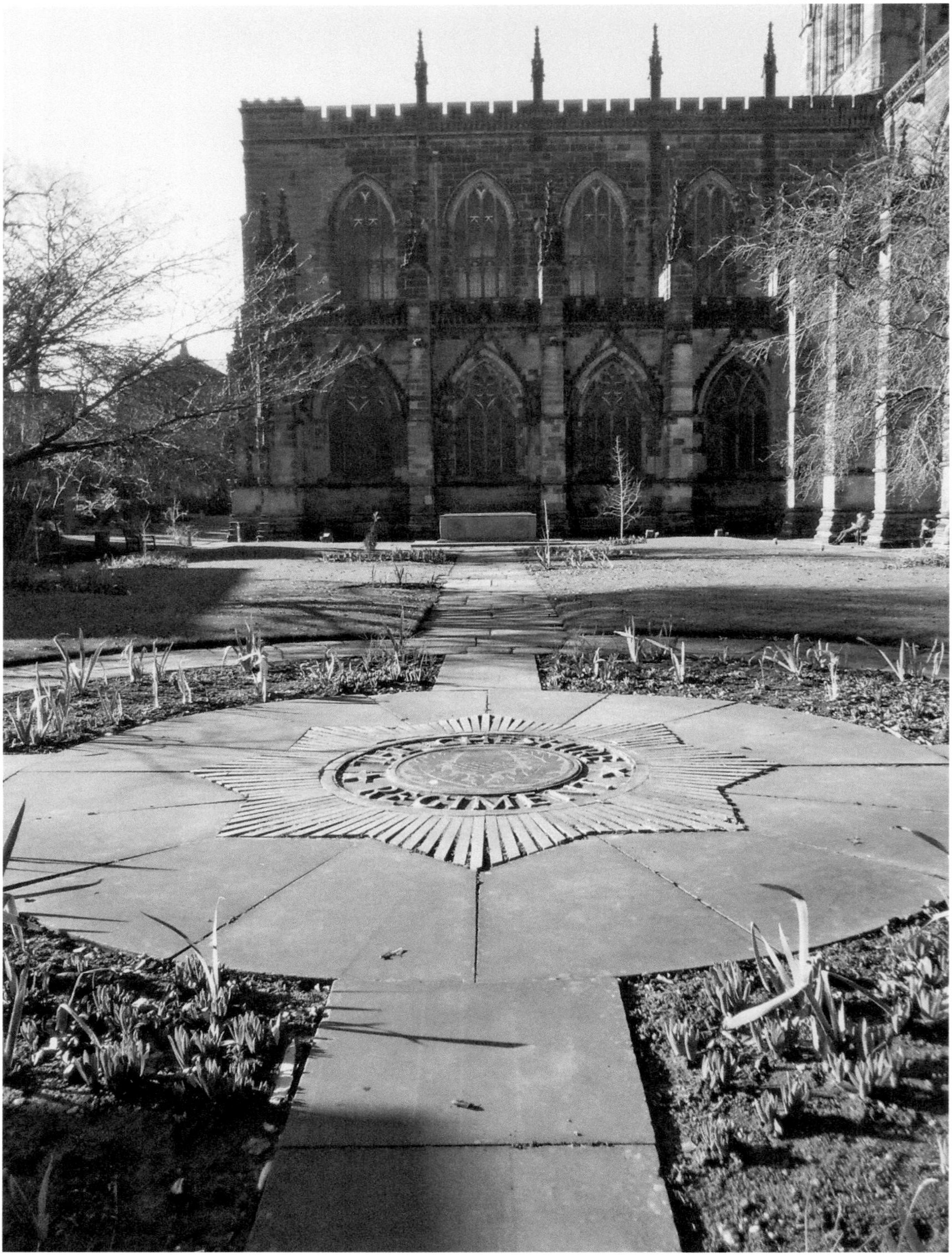

Cheshire Regiment Memorial Garden, Chester Cathedral.

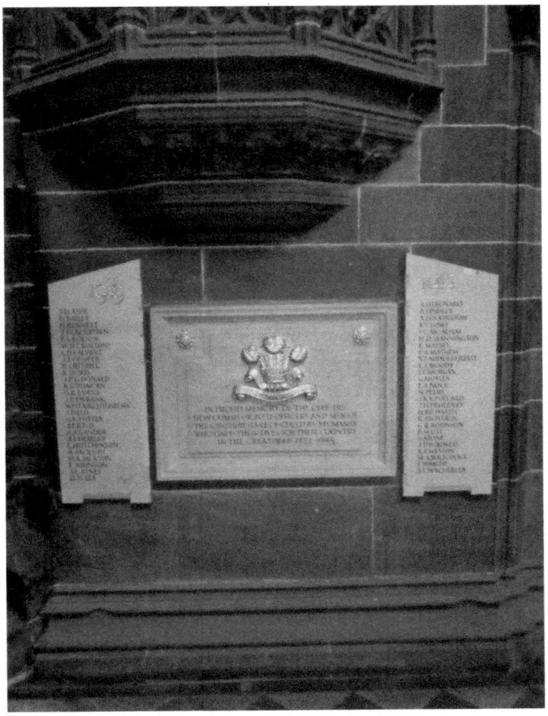

EOCY Second World War Memorial,
Chester Cathedral.

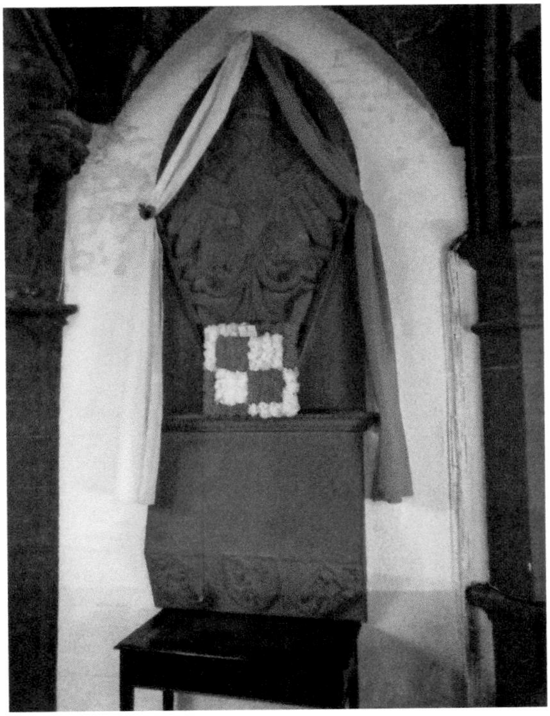

Chester Town Hall Polish War Memorial.

Bibliography

Bishop, P., *Bomber Boys: Fighting Back 1940–1945* (Harper Press, 2007)

Bishop, P., *Fighter Boys: Saving Britain 1940* (Harper Perennial, 2004)

Burns, Michael G., *Bader: The Man and His Men* (Cassell, 1998)

David, S., *Victoria's Wars: The Rise of Empire* (Penguin, 2006)

Fitzhardinge, L. F., *Australian Dictionary of Biography*, Vol. 2 (Melbourne University Press, 1967)

Fraser, A., *The Weaker Vessel: Woman's Lot in Seventeenth-Century England* (Mandarin, 1989)

Holmes, Richard, *Redcoat: The British Soldier in the Age of Horse and Musket* (Harper Collins, 2001)

Hurley, P., *Chester in 50 Buildings* (Stroud: Amberley Publishing, 2019)

Lewis, C. P. & A. T. Thacker (eds), *A History of the County of Chester: Vol. 5 Pt. 1, The City of Chester: General History and Topography* (London: Victoria County History, 2003)

Montgomery, B. L., *A Concise History of Warfare* (Collins, 1972)

Plant, D., *bcw-project.org* (2001–15)

Royden, M., *Chester at War* (Stroud: Amberley Publishing, 2019)

Stuart, E., *What did you do in the War, Deva?* (Chester City Council, 2005)

Acknowledgements

The authors would like to express their particular thanks to Alex Clark, and all the staff at the Cheshire Military Museum, for allowing access to the many invaluable artefacts and exhibits under their control. In addition, the authors would like to thank Corey Estenson for her illuminating talk on the origins of the Earl of Chester's Yeomanry (delivered at the Weaver Hall Museum, Northwich, on 21 September 2019) and the many libraries, archives and museums around the world who have allowed us access to their varied photographic collections. Finally, we would like to thank the private photographers whose publically available images have been of considerable use in the production of this book. Every effort has been made to fulfil requirements with regard to copyright matters. The authors and publisher will be glad to rectify any omissions at the earliest opportunity.

About the Authors

Adrian Bridge was born at Bucklow Hill, near Knutsford, Cheshire, and has taught military and political history at various FE and HE institutions across the country since the 1980s. Since retiring as a senior history lecturer, Adrian has written extensively on both educational and historical issues and continues to work as a senior assessment specialist in history for the Cambridge Assessment wing of the University of Cambridge. Adrian's wife, Dawn, originally from Stoke, moved to Cheshire after completing a history degree, and is a specialist in women's history and genealogical research. She has produced and delivered exhibitions on Hidden Women of Cheshire and has made significant written contributions to the online Amazing Women by Rail project. Both Adrian and Dawn come from families with strong military connections. Adrian's father was a career soldier from Liverpool who fought alongside the Cheshire Regiment in the 1945 assault across the River Rhine. His grandfather was at the Battle of El Alamein, and Adrian's mother was a military nurse who dealt with Second World War POWs returning from the

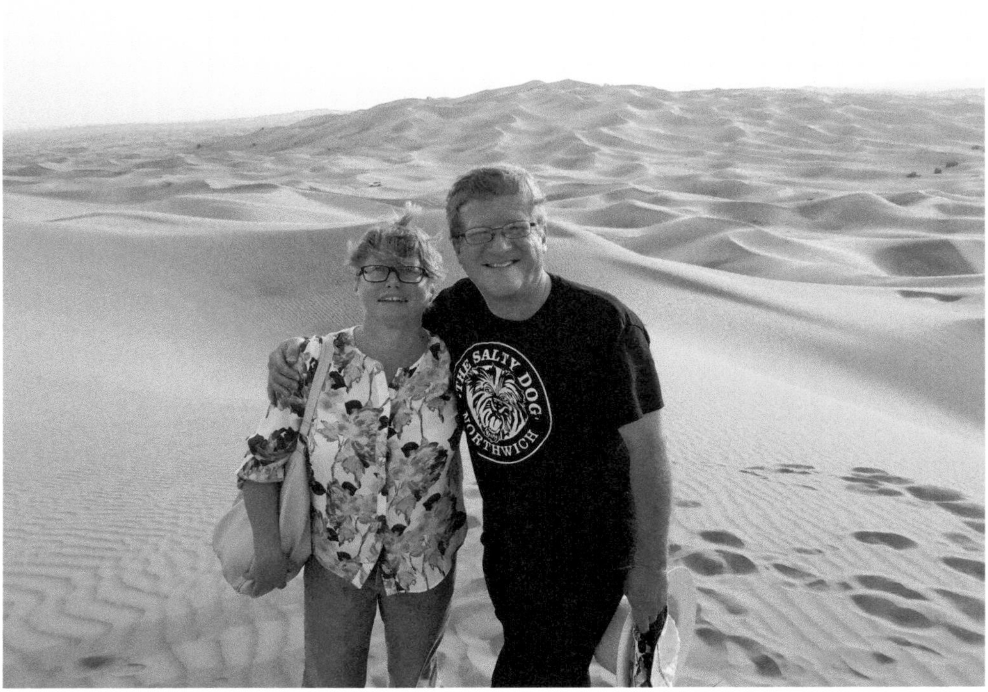

Adrian and Dawn in Dubai, 2018.

Far East. Dawn's great-uncle was a member of the Staffordshire Regiment (now part of the Mercians) who fought at Gallipoli, and was later killed at Arras, on the Western Front, in 1917. Her grandfather was also one of the first British soldiers to land on the beaches of Normandy in 1944. Dawn and Adrian's military connections and memories have made the writing of this book on *Chester's Military Heritage* a particularly enjoyable experience for both writers.

Also by the Same Authors

A–Z of Northwich & Around: People, Places, History (Amberley Publishing, 2019)
Northwich & Around in 50 Buildings (Amberley Publishing, 2021)
Forthcoming:
Secret Northwich & Around (Amberley Publishing)